Under the Music

Collected Prose Poems

Maxine Chernoff

MadHat Press
Asheville, North Carolina

MadHat Press
MadHat Incorporated
PO Box 8364, Asheville, NC 28814

Copyright © 2019 Maxine Chernoff
All rights reserved

The Library of Congress has assigned
this edition a Control Number of
2019931808

ISBN 978-1-941196-85-4 (paperback)

Cover image: *Orpheus* by Odilon Redon (1840–1916)
Cover design by Marc Vincenz
Book design by MadHat Press

www.madhat-press.com

First Printing

Table of Contents

Introduction: Embracing the Ghost
   by Robert Archambeau   xiii

FROM *The Last Aurochs* (1976) & *A Vegetable Emergency* (1977)

The Moat	3
A Vegetable Emergency	5
The Broom	7
In the Moonlight	8
The Annual Picnic	9
High Rise	10
Birth of a Chair	11
The Last Aurochs	12

FROM *Utopia TV Store* (1979)

The Sitting	17
Toothache	18
His Pastime	19
Sailing	20
Water Music	21
The Fan	22
A Lesson in Cause and Effect	23
Fred Astaire	24
Top Hand with a Gun	25
Body and Soul	26
Van Gogh's Ear	27
Phantom Pain	28
Vanity, Wisconsin	29
The Inner Life	30
The World of Ideas	32
Evolution of the Bridge	33
Subtraction	34
Kill Yourself with an *Objet d'Art*	35

The Man Struck Twenty Times by Lightning	36
The Dead-Letter Office	37
Rehearsal	38
The Limits of Science	39
The Fetus	40
A Definition	41
The Boat	42
On My Birthday	43
What the Dead Eat	44
The Meaning of Anxiety	45
An Abridged Bestiary	46
A Birth	47
The Insomniac's Notebook	48
The Horizontal Brigade	50
Utopia TV Store	51
The Shoe and the City	52
A Sense of Humor	53
Anonymous Thoughts from Home	54
The Woman Who Straddled the Globe	56
In the Hospital	57
The Time of the Plague	58
The Stand-up Tragedians	59
New Year's Eve	61

FROM *NEW FACES OF 1952* (1985)

Lost and Found	65
Biographia Literaria	66
The Smell Convention	67
Spring	68
Prophecy	69
A Name	70
Identity Principle	71

PROSE POEMS

Sotto Voce	72
Sayings of my Distant Uncle	73
Miss Congeniality	74
Hairdo	75
Learning to Listen	76
Animal Magnetism	77
How We Went	78
Anger	79
The Edible Harp	80
Beginning, Middle, End	81
The Unzipped	82

FROM *LEAP YEAR DAY : NEW AND SELECTED POEMS* (1990)

How Lies Grow	85
The Apology Store	86
The New Money	88

FROM *WORLD: POEMS 1991–2001* (2001)

Nomads	91
Beauty	92
Heavenly Bodies	94
Wearing Moe	97
Her Many Occupations	100
Guilt	102
Husband and Wife	104
An Epiphany	108
Killing Himself	110
The Method	112
The Sound	116
Wash	119

Uncollected Prose Poems from *Evolution of the Bridge*

Five Possible Moments	123
Origin	125
The Commonplace	126
Quizzing Glass	127
The Unbuilding	128

from *The Turning* (2008)

What It Contains	131
Scenes from Ordinary Life	135
He Picked up His Pen in Her Defense	139

from *Here* (2014)

A House in Summer	147
Daphne	149
Construction	150
Commentary	152
Offerings	156
The Staggering Man	157
Gesture	159
Evidence	161
Anosognosia	163
Parade	165
Aversions	167
Under the Music	169
Purchase	170
Word	171
Singular	172
Drones	174
Stereopticon (3)	175
Beheld	178
Window	179

Momentum	180
Again	181
[untitled]	182
Knowing	183
Philosopher	184
Nocturnal	185
Road	186
Edge	187
Here	188
Nature	189

FROM *CAMERA* (2017)

Preface	193
As If	194
Did I Tell You?	195
Ballad	196
Artifact	197
Cuchulain	198
Acknowledgments	199
About the Author	201

Introduction: Embracing the Ghost

Michael Benedikt (no slouch at the prose poem himself) once wrote that Maxine Chernoff "writes prose poems that are ... as different from the conventional expectations of the genre as certain verse is distant from true poetry." Whatever instinct one has to agree with Benedikt's assessment of Chernoff as standing out from the crowd soon founders on the question of just what our conventional expectations for the prose poem really are—or, indeed, if there are such things as conventional expectations for a genre as nebulous as the one under consideration. Try to grasp it, and the prose poem drifts away, a ghost where you thought you'd find a solid body.

A conventional history of the genre seems, at first, easy enough to put together. It all begins with Aloysius Bertrand's *Gaspard de la Nuit*, begun in 1836 and published in 1842. Things lie fallow until Baudelaire returns to the rich soil Bertrand had tilled, giving us the fifty miraculous little pieces of *Paris Spleen*. From this, a tradition grows in France, the seeds of which travel to the English-speaking world in the translations of French prose poems collected in Stuart Merrill's *Pastels in Prose* in 1890. Soon we reap a harvest in the works of Dowson and the Decadents, Oscar Wilde's 1894 *Poems in Prose* bending the bough with heavy fruit. In the 1920s further infusions of Francophone genius—this time, the translations of Surrealist prose poetry published by Eugene Jolas in *transition*—revived a faltering Anglo-American interest in the genre. The process repeated with a broader internationalist flavor when Robert Bly's translations helped give rise to another wave of prose poetry in English, one that included works by Russell Edson, then Michael Benedikt, then Chernoff herself. This conventional history, though, depends on us believing we know where to draw a boundary around the genre of the prose poem, and, as the *Princeton Encyclopedia of Poetry and Poetics* somewhat sniffily puts it, we have singularly failed to hold fast to any meaningful definition. "The term 'prose poem,'" we may read in that authoritative text, "has been applied irresponsibly to anything from the Bible to a novel by Faulkner."

Our expectations for the prose poem—contra Benedikt—have been as variable as our definitions from the earliest attempts to formulate them on. In the letter on prose poetry Baudelaire wrote to his editor Arsène Houssaye, so often published along with *Paris Spleen,* he tells us the prose poem is essentially lyric and expressive of inner states, reflecting "the lyrical impulses of the soul, the undulations of reverie, the jibes of conscience." But he also tells us that it is in essence narrative and mimetic, focused on the external world of life in metropolises, reflecting "the medley of their innumerable interrelations." Perhaps it shouldn't surprise us that Baudelaire's letter points in contradictory directions: the prose poem is, as any number of wags have observed, like tragicomedy, in that to utter its name is to speak an oxymoron.

Some critics have followed Baudelaire's first line of thought, defining the prose poem as different from other prose by virtue of its expressive lyricism, a theory that does not withstand contact with Russell Edson's work, nor with many of the more narrative pieces in the present volume. Others have looked to narrative as the essence of the genre, but have had difficulty in drawing distinctions between the prose poem and short-short stories, parables, fables, and other established short prose genres. Even the generally reliable M. H. Abrams fumbles when trying to define the form and our expectations for it, saying it differs from other prose genres by virtue of an insistently rhythmic musicality—a claim that looks good if we read, say, Chernoff's "Lost and Found," but not when we turn a few more pages and read on. Is it any wonder that one of the most perennial lines of thinking about the prose poem has maintained that we should rid ourselves of the concept entirely? T. S. Eliot said there was poetry and there was prose, and would have no truck with any strange hybrid; decades later the scholar Stephen Fredman argued that the prose poem signaled a kind of apocalypse, pointing to the end of genre entirely. The Germans have never had any patience for the notion of the prose poem: there term for those things we call by that name translates simply as "short prose," no poetry about it.

Yet the prose poem persists. And if we can't agree on any consistent set of expectations for the genre, perhaps we can do better by dividing the genre into sub-catgeories, as Donna Stonecipher does in her remarkable study *Prose Poetry and the City,* where, surveying the terrain, she divides the empire of the prose poem into two provinces.

On the one hand, there's the Baudelairean: poems that make heavy use of narrative structures and that bear more than a passing resemblance to short-short stories of flash fiction, such as those of Russell Edson; on the other there's the Rimbaudian: surrealistic or dreamlike collections full of unlikely, or unexplained, juxtapositions, such as the prose poems of Rosmarie Waldrop.

Michel Delville, in his indispensable 1998 study *The American Prose Poem,* classes Maxine Chernoff's prose poetry with the first, Baudelarean or Edsonian form of prose poetry, which he calls the "fabulist" school. This, he says, is narrative-based stuff, often with an element of the parable and, in Chernoff's case, tending to extend a metaphor or conceit in an almost Jacobean fashion. He's right, too—but only with regard to the prose poetry available to him at the time he wrote. If we consider the first poem from the present collection, we can see what he means. "The Dead Letter Office" is no lyric effusion, but a story, albeit an odd one, depending less on realism's metonymy than on an extension of the metaphor inherent in the idiom "dead letter"—sorrow, drawn drapes, hankies, morticians all make an appearance in the opening sentences:

> Wistfulness covers the windows like drapes. Ten men, armed with hankies, sort the mail into two categories: letters that make them happy, letters that make them sad. Don't get me wrong. These civil servants, trusted with the awesome duty of burning millions of letters a year, do not open the envelopes, like a mortician prying into the life of a client.

"And what bliss," we read later, at the end of the poem, "when something intervenes and a doomed letter, like a terminally ill patient, is saved." Chernoff returns to the idea of a letter's death as insistently as Donne returns to the notion of lovers as the legs of a compass.

If we fast-forward to the last prose poem in this book, though, written long after Delville published his scholarly volume, we find something altogether different at work.

> The story, written in leaves, is of distance and turning. How to exit by means of a season without the sharp folding of a paper notion? Reliquary and shadow box dance a brief tango to how we

meant paint but simply said black. And acres are burning in driest September, goodbye to all that, a condition of matter. Say water and the box remains empty. Light beams on the surfeit.

If there's a story here, it is elliptical, deliberately omitting cues and connections. What it has, instead, are the unlikely and unexplained juxtapositions Stonecipher sees in the prose poetry of Rosmarie Waldrop. The leaps from one section to another aren't baseless: we move from turning and leaves to seasons, from leaves (presumably foliage) to another kind of leaves (folded paper pages). But the connections are remote, or oblique, or made as if with the sliding logic of a Surrealist film montage or a dream. It can be difficult, in this context, even to know what part of speech we are looking at: does light beam in a complete sentence at the end, or are we looking at a fragment in which beams of light are "on the surfeit"? This particular prose poem invites exactly this kind of unknowing.

One way, then, to view Maxine Chernoff's body of work in prose poetry is to see it as a journey from the first sort of prose poetry outlined by Stonecipher—narrative and Edsonian—to the second sort, dreamlike, elliptical, Waldropian. But like so many claims about prose poetry, this proves too simple and clear-cut for such a various genre. It omits, for example, Chernoff's whole turn toward the expressive first person, something carefully excluded from so many of the early prose poems, but richly evident in *New Faces of 1952*.

What, then, are we holding when we pick up a collection of Maxine Chernoff's achievements in the prose poem form? If not a collection of fables, or a collection of first-person lyrics without lines, or a collection of elliptical dreams—one filmless *Un Chien Andalou* after another—what do we have, exactly? What binds them together, except for the publisher's stitching or glue? In the end, it is an act of affiliation with the whole, complex, contradictory heritage of the prose poem's tradition that comes to the fore. The refusal of lineation is, like the use of lineation in more conventional poems, a signifier, directing us to a context against which the work before us can be read. And more than any other significant practitioner of the prose poem form, Maxine Chernoff embraces the whole breadth of that tradition.

—Robert Archambeau

FROM *THE LAST AUROCHS* (1976)
& *A VEGETABLE EMERGENCY* (1977)

The Moat

Two soldiers, masquerading as trees, pass me casually on the street. Aware of the possibility that they're armed, I avert my eyes, questioning their peculiar disguise only to myself. I walk on only to come upon two trees dressed as soldiers.

I assume that the soldiers and trees have made an even exchange, and aware of the possibility that the trees, was easily as the soldiers could be armed, walk directly toward my home.

Arriving there just after dark, I see that the drawbridge has been raised. I compare my situation to that of a piece of luncheon meat destined for a sandwich, only to discover that the bread it was supposed to occupy is no longer available.

I question the possibility of swimming the narrow width of the channel. Stripping to the waist, I notice how my skin catches the eerie glow of the moon, making me look terribly anemic. This hypochondriacal observation adds to my reluctance about attempting the swim.

I empty my pockets to make the load lighter and leave their contents—some coins, a key, and a ticket stub—inside of my boot on the bank. As I submerge myself in the dark water, I find that all I can think about are blue, shiny plums. Despite my mind's obsession, I find my arms and legs moving rhythmically. If they were statesmen, they would be articulate speakers.

Shivering, I lift myself out of the water and knock vigorously on the door. James, the butler, opens the door. He is surprised to see me partially undressed. His reaction triggers in me, for the first time this evening, the realization that I am a woman, and for the first time in his employment with me, that he is a man. Bowing graciously, he hands me a dry, white towel.

Maxine Chernoff

I question the servants and find that not one of them knows why the bridge was raised before I returned home. Satisfied with this answer, I settle down for the evening. My tea, hot and fragrant as ever, is brought to me, and I retire to read a rather obscure book of aphorisms, comfortably wrapped in my white wool shawl, iridescent in the moonlight.

A Vegetable Emergency

There is something new among the vegetables in my garden this morning, a sinister weed with brown hair-like filaments. I start tugging but find it surprisingly resilient. Bracing myself like a sailor hoisting anchor in a gale, I nearly fall over backwards.

The ground gives way to the head of a man, attractive, about forty, with brown wavy hair. A small white butterfly, straying from the cabbage patch, has landed above his ear. I picture Gauguin arriving in Tahiti in much the same way, a startled islander pulling him from the rhubarb-colored sand. But a head seems to be all that exists of this man. I wonder what he's doing in my garden, a city plot smaller and less enticing than even the Paradise Lounge down the street. I ask him this, but he stares off at the white fence, stony and mute.

I wonder if the head, like a hangnail, is a little-discussed but nevertheless common occurrence. I consult manuals, finding only parasites, fungi, and frost among the vegetable emergencies. No mention of a head, obtrusive as a fireplug in a desert. I call a few neighbors for advice. They are sympathetic but noncommittal.

That night I sit in bed, watching fireflies circling the jar-like head. I wonder what will happen when fall comes and I've eaten or canned all the crops. I imagine plowing up the garden, burying the head under a mound of earth and hoping for an early blizzard. But what if the head resurfaced each year, perhaps doubled in size, edging the other vegetables far from the sunlight? One blow from my spade might dispatch it abruptly as it arrived. But what if it screamed? A head so obstinately silent might be absolutely vociferous. Unable to sleep, I listen to the crickets as if to canned laughter.

Over my morning coffee, I distractedly read the newspaper. Outside my window, the head, like a silent Mafia don, dominates the garden.

Maxine Chernoff

A sale at the greenhouse resolves the problem for me: by 10 a.m., I've purchased a dozen geranium plants. Like an expert milliner, I artfully cover the head with pink and orange flowers. Fuzzy begonia leaves patch closed the relentless eyes. I hang the *For Sale* sign in front of the house and wait for a prospective buyer. I hope, in its cloister of leaves, the head has vowed silence.

The Broom

The broom was angry with the shoe. For two days without success, it had tried to remove the shoe from under the bed. Its long, deft strokes reminded one of a child prodigy playing a harp. The brown shoe perched in the farmost corner, snug as a cat on a ledge.

The broom realized there were possibilities for extricating the shoe that excluded its use. Then what would become of the broom? Was it to pick up token crumbs dropped by a housewife solicitous of its welfare? The broom knew this was no fairy tale. It couldn't stretch to tremendous heights, like Jack's famed beanstalk, or grow wrinkled and gray, like the trunk of a cartoon elephant.

That night, when the woman placed the broom in its usual corner, it did not lean to the right like a drunk in a doorway. It stood stiff and erect as a misbehaved schoolboy proud of his banishment from a class of inferiors. "Come morning the self-important shoe and the placating woman will learn a thing or two," thought the broom. It felt a charge of strength glow through its long bristles like electric current.

In the Moonlight

The horse hears a rustling as flies asleep in his long sleek tail swirl around like sparks in the wind. The sunflower, still closed, dreams of its forthcoming yellow.

I wake to find the room filled with light. The walls pulse silently as twenty hearts, above and below me, beat in unison. The bubbling of the fish tank is the only sound, rubbing the edges of the room.

Bored, I think of a means of escape: to walk on window ledges, stepping carefully to avoid all shadows, where darkness is stored in huge vats.

Then like a cat, I'd jump from a great height and land gently on my feet, as a maple seed lands after being blown through two states.

The Annual Picnic

Fire has gone to a picnic. Carefully, it spreads its iridescent blanket next to a family of four.

The children notice it first, swarming around the blanket like moths.

In the middle of the softball game, the adults detect a gray silence, heavy as a down parka, covering the afternoon.

Like an auctioneer, Fire holds their attention.

A slight woman, delegated by the refreshment committee, congenially extends a paper cup of lemonade into the swirling mass.

Two representatives sign Fire up for the three-legged race.

Finally, it is evening. The gray buses plod out of the gates.

Fire sleeps under a nearby tree, drunkenly satisfied with the summer outing.

High Rise

The man next door has extended a long wooden plank out of his window. Twenty-six floors above the city, I watch him every night. With the certainty of a commuter train, he arrives at eight o'clock. He always dresses in orange trunks and black flippers. A white towel drags majestically behind him. He bends at the waist, extends his long arms, swan-like, and springs up and down three times. He never loses his footing.

Later in the evening, he and his wife enjoy a stroll to the edge of the plank. Hand in hand they sit facing each other. Then like hungry birds they open their cavernous mouths and look straight up at the sky. Often they sit there for hours, still as a bowl of fruit on a table.

When the woman leaves around midnight, the man performs his closing ritual. He braces himself with his legs and throws his head back with such force that the plank moans hideously. He closes his eyes and howls once in the voice of a strange animal.

The stars turn over in their graves of sky.

Birth of a Chair

The tree cannot be left by means of tree.
—Francis Ponge

The chair spoke to the table. "Table, I have watched man for years. I am ready to become one." Silent as usual, the table's grainy wood gleamed in the sun. It had no secrets and was satisfied.

The owner of the chair noted a change from that day. As he sat in it, he could almost hear it say, "I'm bored," or "Rainy days make me ache." The man was practical and credited himself with a new sensitivity to things around him. He polished the chair dutifully and never spilled gravy on the reticent table.

One day the chair awoke feeling particularly energetic. "Let's play a game," it said to the table. It had, by now, developed quite a full imagination. Earnestly it tumbled across the room. First a leg broke off, then another, then its seat clattered to the ground like a basket of broken eggs.

By now the man had come home from work. Seeing the remains of the chair, he felt relieved, for his sensitivity was becoming a strain. He carried it out to the garbage. The chair heaved a sigh and spoke to the garbage can. "Garbage can, I have watched man for years. I am ready to become one."

"That is foolish," said the garbage can and fell asleep.

Maxine Chernoff

The Last Aurochs

Father wears antlers to dinner, antlers so large that his head resembles a small tree in winter. We no longer look at each other but just keep eating. Mother doesn't seem to notice it anymore. She told us to treat Father as if nothing had happened. That was hard at first. So much had been in the papers. It was all they talked about in town. You see, Father destroyed the tourist trade. In fact, he destroyed the only commerce in town other than cows, the museum where the last aurochs was displayed.

The last aurochs, ancestor of our modern cow, died in Poland in 1627. The people in that little town donated its bones and a few artifacts to our town as a goodwill gesture about ten years ago. Because Father fought there during the war, they made him curator of the museum. He kept the bones in a glass case, the tarnished bell on the door, and the water trough and feed bag, always filled with water and the freshest alfalfa, in the middle of the room. Since there were no pictures of the aurochs, we had to imagine how it looked: furrier and larger than our cows today with sadder eyes and a nobler glance.

Father loved his job. He wouldn't have intentionally burned down that museum if his life depended on it. The fire started because he cared too much. When he'd come home, Mother would ask him if he'd had a good day. He'd always say that he had, that tourists had come, that he'd rung the aurochs bell for them. Nothing he said explained his drawn face or his red, swollen eyes. We could never understand his sadness until one night when we heard some commotion in the back yard.

We all ran to the window and saw Father prancing around in the moonlight, wearing those huge antlers. It was a beautiful dance, a dance in which Father expressed the longing that the last aurochs must have felt for a companion. It was a mating dance that bulls in our country still do today. It went on until the sun came up.

Father never mentioned it to us. He'd come to breakfast looking drowsy and quietly leave for work. Soon he didn't even care about his uniform. His shirt was dirty. He lost buttons. The dance went on night after night. He perfects a series of cries that went along with it. Pathetic mooing, guttural, low.

Now Mother looked worn too. She was worried. One night there were two aurochs out in the back yard, Father, and Mother, wearing antlers somehow implanted in her hairdo. She copied his dance but did it more gracefully. She answered his calls in a voice so sweet that we nearly cried. But in the middle of the dance, just at the point when it touched us most, something strange happened. Father screamed, "It's a lie! They aren't extinct! It's a lie." He walked in the house and had his first sound sleep in weeks.

Father started going to work later and later. The museum suffered from his lack of interest. One night a pile of old papers went up in flame. The museum burned before we could save the tarnished bell or a single bone. Since then Father won't speak to Mother. He won't take off his antlers and he won't even say the word cow. Sometimes I see him sending off letters. He addresses them to that town in Poland. Every day the mail comes. There is no reply. Every now and then he moans sadly, watching the tall grass swaying in the yard.

FROM *Utopia TV Store* (1979)

The Sitting

> On November 8, 1895, W. C. Roentgen took a picture of his wife's hand. His mysterious rays became widely known by the mysterious letter X, but some of their significant properties became known only later. Meanwhile, enterprising photographers established "Roentgen studios," and did a lively business in x-ray sittings.

The line forms early each Sunday. Pregnant women bring their just-formed infants. Lovers are x-rayed in an embrace, creating a confusion of bone. One old man, wearing all black, says that he's come for a portrait of his hands folded in death. A well-dressed family waits stiffly in line. The mother adjusts her daughter's ample ears, as if they were taffy or bonsai branches. Men ogle the x-ray portrait of a well-known courtesan.

"No two are alike," says the x-ray photographer. His thin, aesthetic hands hold up framed x-rays: the men of the Academy, a dog who swallowed a key. A man milking his prize cow. The Queen Mother. Feathery shadows: even the fat lady is finely chiseled by the benevolent rays.

As evening comes, the studio empties. The x-ray machine, nostalgic as a general on an empty battlefield, hums on into the night.

Toothache

I never had a toothache, but the desire to have one crossed my mind constantly. Thinking a toothache was starting, I consulted a doctor who attributed to the pain to a small insect bite on the left tonsil. From that day I abandoned the hope of ever feeling a quick stab of pain or a steady musical throbbing. My teeth were a fortress against any invaders, the health spa of an otherwise decrepit body.

Sometimes I'd see a person rubbing his fingers over a spot on his cheek hot as a sidewalk in summer. Envious, I'd fall off chairs, steps, and bicycles, trying to land on my mouth. I took up meditation and biofeedback to focus some pain in my teeth. Like children, bored with the gifts of a visiting aunt, they remained uninvolved.

Finally, quite by chance, I found a way to bring myself relief. Through a new medical procedure, the dentist removed one healthy tooth and planted a large, decaying molar in its place. It was worth the trouble. Now, when I pass a candy store, I buy the chewiest caramels. And when I crunch on an ice cube, the pain is long and complex as a medieval tapestry.

His Pastime

A man held his breath. Unlike other men who momentarily hold their breath, then gasp like small bags bursting, this man continued for days. He stopped working and gave up all nourishment. His face turned blue as a police uniform, then black. Even his shadow held its breath, motionless on the floor.

A newspaper heard of this man, perched on his breath like a flagpole. They sent a reporter to cover the story. The man holding his breath served the reporter cookies and tea. In response to the reporter's first question, the man politely exhaled. His breath, like a funnel, upturned all the things in the room.

Unimpressed, the reporter lifted himself from under his chair and cracked teacup. The next day on his way to work, the man who had held his breath read an editorial decrying swindlers, fanatics, and thrill-seekers.

Sailing

Benjamin Franklin used to lie naked on the water, attack a kite to his leg, and let the wind gently carry him around the pond like a sailboat. On days when the weather was especially pleasant, you could hear him talking to himself above the jabber of the various pond creatures. In this liquid medium he wrote his clever epigrams. He explained that the water actually spoke to him in sentences, thus inventing the concept of *onomatopoeia*.

One rainy night he met with near disaster when lightning struck the tail of his kite. The electric current traveled through his body, setting his wooden teeth aflame. For a week he lay unconscious, a jack-o'-lantern grin behind his badly blistered gums.

Water Music

In his last years, Beethoven, deaf and worn by poverty, thought that he heard his own works everywhere. Chairs hummed his overtures, tables were tympani joining on cue, and teapots whistled the opening of the *Fifth*. His grandson would hold a conch shell to Beethoven's ear and he would exclaim, "Ach, Gott! Mein *Pastorale!*"

The bewildered child matured, convinced that his grandfather was correct. He tried to claim ownership of all sea shells. On the 20th of each month, regardless of the weather, he went to the ocean to hear the starfish, sea urchin, and anemone join in a chorus of *An Die Freude*.

He began inviting important personages to his grandfather's music. On the morning after one such event, certain articles were found floating on the water. A monocle on a black velvet string, a periwig with faint traces of white powder, and a silver conductor's baton were all that remained of the seven dukes, five duchesses, and earl known to attend.

Authorities concluded that the audience had drowned, carrying their chairs into the surf to hear the piccolo solo in Beethoven's *Ninth*.

The Fan

I enter a room where a fan seems to be chanting "Air! Air! Air!" as it whirs. I see it's not a fan, after all, but a child facing the wall in the far corner of the room.

At the opposite end of the room, a man is seated, stroking his beard. He keeps repeating, "Yes, quite excellent. Air wafers. Air wafers."

I turn off the fan, and the child and man stop instantly, as if slapped in the face.

A Lesson in Cause and Effect

While staring in the mirror, a man shrugged his shoulders Outside his window a tree bobbed up and down as if floating upright on water. Confused, he shrugged his shoulders again. The plates from his cabinet spun on the floor like huge dimes. He turned on the radio. He couldn't tune in a station so he shrugged his shoulders. His neighbors wobbled on their lawns like bowling pins after a strike.

The man knew his place in the universe, always comparing himself to the lowly ant. He was parsimonious, and whenever he heard a boast, he glared angrily. Yet now it seemed that the movement of his shoulders was directly proportional to the disaster around him. He was puzzled and unconsciously shrugged his shoulders. A large brass vase fell from the mantle, hitting him squarely on the head. He teetered for a moment, then spun to the ground like a child's top unwinding..

Outside it was silent. The whole universe, or what was left of it, waited for him to revive.

Fred Astaire

Ever since he danced on the ceiling in *Royal Wedding*, he hasn't been the same. There is a longing, a profound blush that starts in his toes and seizes the ankles. It is a feeling so intense that he must dash out of cabs, forgetting to tip his invisible top hat to passing ladies. Then, exhausted, he rests on a bench, feet tapping uncontrollably. Movies are impossible for Mr. Astaire to attend. No sooner is he seated than he begins to turn objects upside down: popcorn rolls down the aisle, Cokes splash like buckets of dirty water. During his last interview, Mr. Astaire turned his leather chair over and proceeded to straddle its broad most part as if riding a buffalo. His wife smiled knowingly. His granddaughter ran in shouting, "Grandpa, Grandpa! Pick me up!" Astaire took firm hold of the child's calves and held her like a double-handled mop, hair lightly brushing the ground. At moments like these one sees an incredible transformation in Astaire's features. The deep wrinkles, engraved like monograms in fine silver, disappear. His blue eyes focus on the peak of his slanted roof and nestle there like doves.

Top Hand with a Gun

Top Hand with a Gun begins. A seat away from me a man loudly chews popcorn. To silence him I shout "Fire!" but no one moves. As I look around the theater, I see all the people in the movie. There's the blonde girl, her bonnet pinker than a baby's tongue. The heavy man in black is showing her card tricks. His hands move deftly as bats. Amorphous, the townspeople sit together. One by one they are gunned down on screen. The heavy man's oily lips spread as the number of bodies increases. Suddenly the screen is white and lights illumine the theater. The cast shuffles out. As I leave, people wait in line for the next performance. The heavy man shoots randomly into the crowd. Men and women scream and fall. Then a single shot is fired. Like an overstuffed chair dropped from an attic window, the heavy man rolls to one side. The survivors wait calmly in line, clutching their tickets serenely as prayer books.

Body and Soul

The day I drowned began like any other. I turned off the alarm clock and turned over in bed. My dreams had, once again, been of poached eggs, my usual breakfast. That morning I was in a hurry. The wind was from the east, as I had hoped. My ability to foretell its direction was strong as a bear's instinct to wake with the first whiff of spring.

The men of the village, dressed as trees and bushes to facilitate hunting, were up with the sunrise. From them I had learned to wear the suit of a fish when setting sail. For years I had dragged the heavy costume down to the water's edge, marking a zigzag pattern behind me. The suit had become frayed at the fins, as an old bag of flour leaks first at the seams. Struggling into the costume, the tight rubbery scales reassured me. Once on, it fit comfortably as old pajamas.

I floated far from shore, the water sounding distant as someone else's heartbeat. Suddenly I felt a small bead of coldness, as if someone had shot me in a fingertip or an earlobe. This was my last memory before the fishermen caught me the next day. Elated at finding such a large fish, they carried me carefully from the boat. I felt a perverse pride that my fish costume had been so convincing to trained eyes.

When I was displayed in the marketplace, a few friends recognized my costume. To save the fishermen from humiliation, they bought me on the pretense of serving me to the village at the next religious festival. Had it been possible, I would have favored the alternative. Instead, they waited until night to peel the rubbery skin from me. They floated my costume, gleaming silver in the moonlight, out to sea, while I, a dark stone, watched coldly from shore.

Van Gogh's Ear

At the exhibit, the ear hangs next to *Bedroom at Arles*. A normal ear in every way, but luminous, like a flat pearl button. The lobe is the size of a thumbprint and whiter, more pulpy, than the rest of the ear. People walk past. Some gasp, some smirk, some sidle up and whisper furtively into it. One man looks awed, recreating the moment when Gauguin received it with the morning mail. The museum had to pay large sums to purchase the ear from its owner, a doctor in Holland, who had kept it on his desk as a paperweight. This is the first public showing, and reviews have been splendid. Rubber copies of the ear are being sold at the counter. If you look closely, you can see they are exact replicas, complete to the fine red down studding the earlobe.

Phantom Pain

After the leg is lost, the pain remains as an emblem; so the kidnapper cannot part with his ransom notes. The high diver, lost on the subway, flexes his muscles defensively. The crowd fades to waves in a pool eighty feet below. "There," pointing to the nose of a seated passenger, "is where I'll land." The mad bomber turns to his wife and says, "I'll give up my career for you." She pictures his delicate bombs defusing like scenes in a home movie played backwards. Meanwhile, the kidnapper, grown careless with sentimentality, drops a ransom note on the subway seat. The train conductor, who last night dreamed of a murderer, hides the note like a stolen pistol, under his cap. Later the bomber stops at a diner full of known bombers. Anxious, he drops a coffee cup, white fragments exploding at his feet.

Vanity, Wisconsin

Firemen wax their mustaches at an alarm. Walls with mirrors are habitually saved. At the grocery, women in line polish their shopping carts. Children too will learn that one buys meat the color of one's hair, vegetables to complement the eyes. There is no crime in Vanity, Wisconsin. Shoplifters are too proud to admit a need. Punishment, the dismemberment of a favorite snapshot, has never been practiced in modern times. The old are of no use, and once a year at their "debut," they're asked to join their reflections in Lake Leblanc. Cheerfully they dive in, vanity teaching them not to float. A visitor is not embarrassed to sparkle here or stand on his hotel balcony, taking pictures of his pictures.

Maxine Chernoff

The Inner Life

for Tymoteusz Karpowicz

After they decreed the end of lovemaking, we thought only of sleeping. Under our covers, each separate as a masthead at sea, we practiced dreaming. For it was the source of our only comfort, our only ties with emotions hazy as deceased uncles. Now we dreamed desperately. Those who couldn't remember their dreams became insurance risks, showing up frequently in the papers as suicides or crime statistics. We were advised to look for mates who appeared to be affluent dreamers: heavy eyelids, an avid indifference to appearance, lights out early, very early, in bedroom windows.

You may be surprised we took mates at all, but we still grew lonely and wanted something to touch even if it vanished when we opened our eyes. Those who excelled at dreaming were chosen to represent us. The forty-hour week was replaced by the forty-hour sleep. It was through our "sleep experience" that we earned advancement at work. New television shows featured dream phantoms to replace late-night horror shows, falling dreams instead of daily soap operas and flying dreams for children. Who succumbed to the old feeling of helplessness when the paraphernalia for heroism was stored in every brain? Soon even our buildings were designed to resemble pillows, and our young ones judged intelligent not by how soon they spoke the hackneyed "Mama," but by how accomplished they were at sleeping. Intelligence tests were given to determine what they could sleep through, and our prodigies withstood avalanches easily as the cracking of porcelain thimbles.

As with all major changes in civilization, the historians were at first puzzled. Many had retired to rest homes where they dreamed the rebuilding of the Roman Empire, the finding of a lost continent, the absence of Hitler. We had lost all sense of nationalism and all instinct for aggression. *One man, one pillow* became the slogan, and even the most impoverished seemed satisfied. Some awake even part of the day suspected that the government had foreseen the outcome. Certain extremists refused to dream, claiming their unconscious was a tool in a scheme more diabolical than Manifest Destiny. But from the solid white building that stood impalpable as a dream image of a building, we heard no denial of the charges, just the assured snoring of men in serious pajamas.

Maxine Chernoff

The World of Ideas

Located in the shadow of *Reader's Digest* Headquarters in Pleasantville, New York, is the World of Ideas. Its brochure claims that it contains "the fallout of cerebral mushroom clouds," "the stunts of acrobatic synapses." There to the left, for example, is the idea of a perfect line, muscular in its daring. There near the window are the portraits of the museum's founders, twins whose heads brush the frames like helium balloons.

I spoke to the museum's director, whose IQ was embroidered in sequins on his blazer. He showed me the splendid catalogue of holdings: photos of angels' weddings, the dreams of mahogany, theories of invisible food, all classified alphabetically. Then he delivered the usual plea for donations:

Explorations must be made into the diaphanous folds of brain tissue, those accordion pleats filled with the dust of spontaneity. Only with the support of a concerned public can the absorption rate of roseate glow in a field of Stradivarius violins be calculated in inverse relation to the consumption rate of a radium ice skate by a pack of hungry chromosomes.

On the way out, much moved by the speech, I place a generous contribution in the 30-foot spittoon, which is the idea of a genius's reflection. Outside, I noticed how the museum was engulfed in a pink smoke haze generated by the tuba-shaped chimney. Had it been there when I entered? Or had The World of Ideas, even as I stood within its walls, acquired a valuable addition to its collection? Perhaps an instant one, purchased with my donation—there is no limit to the speed of thought, you know.

Evolution of the Bridge

Guaranteed in every model is a lifespan shorter than your own. The bridge of wet gardenias is a designed as a study in pathos. Citizens weep past the flowery rails. Commuters are accustomed to detouring at the string-bean bridge. What can provide a better excuse for your late arrival at work? The boss, himself unable to cross the rubber-band drawbridge, will praise your good sense in the matter, promote you to district manager. It is true that a foolhardy sort met his demise on the bridge of pancakes, but that is the only recorded fatality. Consider the greater good. Towns have sprung up around these passing fancies. A village thrives at the foot of a suspension bridge made of feathers. The colorful plumage draws tourists from miles around. On the green, city fathers have erected a sweet-potato statue of their first mayor. At every rainfall a different citizen is sculpted into prominence. Perishable bridges have also relieved the boredom of scenery. Sunday drives are taken with a new sense of urgency. And optimism is flourishing. No longer do girders shiny as new ideas ridicule our own decline. We are treated to an ever-changing landscape as monuments are blissfully forgotten.

SUBTRACTION

First there was addition, incestuous and pretentious, coupling jackals with jackals, summing sunsets and field mice.
Soon the world was packed as a third-class railway car. We tired of objects desiring us—lenses, doorknobs, cuspidors elbowing between lovers. Scholars developed protective philosophies, claiming they'd die for "breathing space," but what of the common man? His only hope was in the invention of madmen—evaporation chambers, metaphysical vacuums, all of which failed. One day in a schoolroom a slow child with glasses forgot to draw the vertical line of the plus sign and so subtraction was born. *Minus, minus,* we chanted all day, watching our laundry recede from the clothesline.

Kill Yourself with an *Objet d'Art*

Choose a heavy one shaped like (a) your first ride in a car or (b) the Hitchcock leg of lamb, served at dinner to the unsuspecting detective. Or a light *objet d'art,* (c) an ice cube in whose reflection is suggested the history of the subconscious.

Now choose a forehead, yours to be exact. Where your hand intersects the mirror-image forehead, strike the blow. If (a) has been your instrument, you will feel run over but sincere; if you chose (b), you will feel theatrical. (c), as you know, was Freud's preference in moments of despair.

If none of these objects appeal to you, consider the following technique: Serve as executor to a million-idiot. He'll gladly leave you trifles and before you know, you'll be the owner of possibilities: a Max Ernst bed equipped with guillotine, a Picasso whose lips are razorblades, a Goya with personal angels, black and familiar.

Maxine Chernoff

THE MAN STRUCK TWENTY TIMES BY LIGHTNING

I've known him so long I've almost forgotten the first photo he showed me, the helpless orphan in the cloud-like bonnet abandoned in a rainstorm. And the scrapbook: *Boy Struck by Lightning on Little League Field. Teen Struck by Lightning at Graduation Exercise. Bride and Groom Struck by Lightning at Altar—One Dies.*

Extraordinary, yes, but his relationship with lightning, which seems the most personal in nature, no longer astounds me. I sometimes think of lightning as his pushy employer. At other times *he* is the master, lightning the recalcitrant servant. He is the ship, lightning the captain. He is the captain, lightning the challenging sea. He is the countryside, lightning the endless white fence.

Often I wonder whether he's contrived the danger to make his attachments more tender. I must admit I can't think of the speed of lightning without some tears. In this way I'm like the mother of the infant born with a full set of teeth. Night after night she lies awake examining the record books, imagining his dubious future.

"Charlatan," I say on rainy nights, for he's never been struck in my presence. Yet with every weather forecast I fear his loss, knowing I'd miss those singed greetings, those thunderous good-byes.

The Dead-Letter Office

Wistfulness covers the windows like drapes. Ten men, armed with hankies, sort the mail into two categories, letters that make them happy, letters that make them sad. Don't get me wrong. These civil servants, trusted with the awesome duty of burning millions of letters a year, do not open the envelopes like a mortician prying into the life of a client. It is the envelope itself that makes them sad. Childish handwriting scrawled to a deceased aunt makes them weep. A letter from overseas to a wife who has moved, unknown to her husband, creates such tumult that the walls quiver like jelly. Few letters are happy ones, the eviction notice never delivered, the lost bill. But when a happy letter does come into their possession, the men cheer wildly, tear up envelopes, and toss them out the windows, tickertape-fashion. And what bliss when something intervenes and a doomed letter, like a terminally ill patient, is saved.

Rehearsal

So you want to be an orchestra. Start small. Be an instrument first. Hang eighty-eight black and white scarves out to dry on a windy day. If the neighborhood dogs circle mournfully, you are succeeding.

If you are past this step, answer the following: Can fear be your snare drum? Can your windpipe rival the lute? How much do your toes, those angry percussionists, respect authority?

I once knew a woman whose spine was a xylophone. Students came from miles around just to hear her exquisite slump into a chair. That is your competition—can you equal it? Are you a French horn in the fetal position? Do your arms wave passionately, or are they sadly reinforced against desire?

Finally you'll need to be the conductor. Try this: chew seventeen crackers into a microphone, then bow deeply. By now the audience is clapping wildly. Hum the opening bar. The seats are vibrating ever so slightly. The baton is hovering just out of reach like last night's rain.

The Limits of Science

—Is this the home of the parakeet with the mechanical heart?

—Yes. We keep him in a cage insulated against wind, rain, noise, and sun.

—May I photograph him?

—Only when he sleeps. The least surprise, even the innocuous click of a camera, might set off an adverse reaction.

—How is it that the bird received a new heart?

—Bird insurance. Two dollars a year paid for a procedure worth well over six thousand dollars. All to save little Kelly.

—You must be relieved the operation was a success.

—We hate the troublesome bird. It's modern science we love.

Maxine Chernoff

The Fetus

The fetus came up to me. It was a normal fetus—large, translucent head, stumpy arms and legs, a heart resembling a bird's nest visible through the chest cavity. It looked at me imploringly, pointing in its ambiguous way at something on my face. The fetus, it seemed, wanted to touch my glasses. I bent down slowly so as not to startle it. It seemed to take hours, and I realized how low I'd have to bend to accommodate my visitor. The touch of the fetus was the touch of someone groping to turn off an alarm, inept and sleepy and furious all at once. In its small commotion, the fetus knocked my glasses to the floor. I hesitated, not daring to speak, to see what it would do. The blurry fetus looked at me, turned, and left abruptly as it had arrived. I wondered whether it had wanted to wear my glasses for a moment or if its intention had been to touch my eye. When my daughter came home from school, I told her this story. Her eyes strained at mine; they had the same look I've detected when she's being lied to by a stranger.

A Definition

As a monument to beauty, an artist designed a miniature windmill composed of the mustaches of the great. Though their identities have been concealed, it is rumored the work contains the mustaches of Marco Polo, Betsy Ross, Rasputin, and Galileo. The artist scrupulously grooms the windmill every morning before he takes to the hill above town. The wind seems to favor his creation with gentle breezes, and nothing is lovelier than its nonchalant curve through air. Observers often ask the artist to reveal the mustaches' origins. One tourist offered a handsome endowment difficult for a man poor as he to refuse. The response was silence. For beauty must exist without history, anonymous as boredom or glacial ice.

The Boat

for my father

I set out in a boat that is also a birdcage. Or should I say a birdcage that is somewhat a boat? For it more resembled a birdcage: light bamboo bent to meet at the peaked roof, a little swing suspended absentmindedly from the top. There were precedents. I'd heard of the man who went to sea in a fire engine. I imagined the waves wafting against the shiny sides, the urgent bells having nothing to ring for at sea.

How wonderful it was when the wind whistled through the rungs, setting the empty swing in motion. The water was aquamarine and the sky was always there, though I never could name its color. At first the going was perilous; the waves had never known a seaworthy birdcage, this ship without cargo or flags or sails. I instructed the birdcage to be more ship, inspiring it through tales of other vessels, the skyscraper that floated on faith alone. The bamboo seemed more formidable after that, and the sound of the boat returned to me as the sound of the sea allowing my boat to float.

I sometimes had occasion to see other boats, and I saluted politely as we passed the vacationers in pink sunglasses, the rainbow deck chairs, the bustling shuffleboard courts. I felt no jealousy for their luxury, no desire for human companionship, knowing my only companion's bamboo reflection was unique in all the ocean.

As the years passed and the bird less swing rocked slowly at the peak of the ship, I knew how famous we'd be for absolutely nothing, for floating past exotic ports as the ocean wind mingled with our air.

On My Birthday

Words line up like racehorses at a starting gate. Nose to nose they edge toward the climactic period. All want to be part of the last line where the reader's gaze will stop, blink, and refocus like a dutiful traffic light. Where do they come from? Like mushrooms they grow in the dark or in clumsy patches, unsightly as warts. Sometimes I try to scare them away. I tell them stories of the pyromaniac, emphasizing the sting of the match. I speak of oblivion as if it were our corner store or the direction the wind will inevitably blow. I tell them they're no better than laundry hanging on the line—that any minute it will rain. Sometimes I threaten to starve them. They're not afraid. They form a column thin as the row of numbers a child might add. Today I appeal to their sympathy. "It's my birthday. I want peace." In no time they write me a beautiful ode. I casually thank them, hiding a lozenge of guilt in my cheek.

WHAT THE DEAD EAT

For centuries the dead did not eat. But new information convinces us of the dead's only tie to the living, their hunger. The concept of hunger after death shouldn't confound. Nor is it mere innuendo, whispered by those who cling to a last human pleasure like an old coat sleeve. For the dead will tell you that their insatiability is no cause for hope. Let me make matters simple. For those who look forward to death as a final rest, expect a canceled vacation. Even the most pious have turned down heaven for a greasy leg of mutton. Mothers do not hear the sobs of their children. Eulogies are delivered to empty picture frames. For all the dead see are gleaming platters of rolls and fragrant cheeses.

It is told that a certain world leader missed a pot roast so sorely that God in pity granted him a final bite. That is the only way the dead are allowed to eat. Do not expect that favor. Societies have long understood the ritual importance of the condemned's last meal, but not until now has its futility been realized. For the hunger of the dead is life's revenge, and it implicates even the soul: many have pined away for a crust so light, a meringue so airy they could inspire flight.

As a whim a few gluttons and mystics have been excused from the "Great Hunger," a term favored by the dead over the more proper "Reverse Transubstantiation." They rest oblivious as tables. Others, in false hope, take their plates to the grave or go out in an orgy of etiquette, napkins tucked neatly under their chins, salad forks poised in rigor mortis. But authorities admonish: *Do not ask what the dead eat. It is too tragic.*

The Meaning of Anxiety

Can you ever look at yourself again without wanting to swallow a cash register? Try to relax. List the potential murders, the disappearances. See the globe become a balloon held by a careless schoolboy.

Remember the past for reassurance, the lesson in perspective, for instance. How the man in the fedora receded endlessly down the railroad tracks only to reappear in next year's arithmetic book, page two hundred forty-eight. Recall the happy hours spent peekabooing with nothingness in that urinous pink and white year of your birth.

When feeling low, compare your life to that of others less fortunate than yourself. Consider the maker of dolls' voices—lying in bed all day inventing doll dialects, doll monologist, doll witticisms. The occupational hazard—a bone in the ear chronically vibrating like a tuba in a corner of a warehouse. You'd long for a spring in which deafness is a garden dreamed in slow motion.

But you've never understood how another's misery can lighten your own. Don't they exist side by side like cars at a stoplight? Lately yours has become so compelling—a sigh that forms like an icicle; a religion of swallowing; a system of visions and hallucinations widely accepted as currency. And the fatal proof of that condition. Suddenly the mundane appears fearfully beautiful. Your shaky laundry must be folded delicately as spider webs. Your hair grows musically. You yearn to meet others with the same blood type.

A bee in one's bonnet is how it's often described, but today no euphemism will suffice. Outside your window birds fly single file carrying the primary colors of your former life.

Maxine Chernoff

An Abridged Bestiary

for Peter Kostakis

As the story goes, Noah took animals of every kind aboard his famed ark. This, however, was not the case. The aardvark and zebra were the only animals that the concise Noah allowed to join him. "Bears to yaks" be damned!" he shouted when his wife asked permission for her pet monkey to board.

Not recognizing in his single-mindedness the very quality that had endeared Noah to God, she smuggled the monkey onto the ship. This feat was easily accomplished given Noah's preoccupations the forty days that the ship labored on swollen seas. He was revising all known bestiaries, tearing out pages and tossing them overboard with the abandon of a crazed housewife cleaning out her refrigerator. By the end of the voyage, he had written *Noah's Book of Animals,* a two-page pamphlet praising the grace of the aardvark and the wit of the zebra.

Contrary to myth, it was the stowaway monkey, not the fabled dove, who announced the sighting of land. A strong swimmer, the monkey had followed the boat, collecting the pictures that Noah discarded. Once the flood ended, Noah saw the pictures drying on a line suspended between two palms trees in the receding water.

Startled, Noah asked God what it could mean. God admonished Noah for his excessive frugality and blessed the intrepid monkey.

The next morning all the animals were re-created according to the discarded pictures that the monkey had saved for God.

A Birth

We must seek bodies for our children.
　—Osage Indian chant

I can't remember the birth. Cold white rooms, cleanliness the color of nothing. Sometimes a woman dreams that she's given birth to a litter of piglets attached to her breasts like pink balloons. When I look in the crib, there is no baby. When I look on the stove, there is a pot of soup which was not there before. Sometimes there is a mix-up at the hospital. A patient orders French onion soup and receives cream of shrimp. Sometimes there is a mix-up; a woman receives a child who grows up hating her. One night at a theater, quite by surprise, a persons steps out of the screen and sits down beside her. That is her child, she knows. "The soup is ready," my husband repeats. Silently we sit down side by side. Silently we share one bowl and then another.

The Insomniac's Notebook

The insomniac's notebook is filled with the dreams of others: "I dreamed of a baby in a nest." "I dreamed of a tailor pressing photographs." "I dreamed of the only living soldier in an army of decoys."

But we're not convinced. We know of his stethoscope reserved for cold bedroom walls on dreamless nights. We know of his fetish for pillows, whose head depressions seem to him the most scenic valleys.

And so when he says to us, "I dreamed of children linking arms on my birthday cake," we feel only fear. It's not the bulging vein in his neck or the quivering lips, tokens of lies harmless of flies in ice cubes. It is our fear that he will become the dream.

He senses our fear. Writing the dream he wears a gaudy ring, finger humpbacked to seem substantial. Thus his outline sewn in every bed sheet. He lies down motionless. His eyes remain open. It is a moonless night so dark he won't imagine darkness and disappear.

And he doesn't disappear. He gets up, looks at his oversized alarm clock, bells large as doughnuts. Three a.m.

The next day his fatigue embarrasses us. Our fear, we explain, is our hope for him. We have secured his passport. His bags, loaded with night shirts, wait at the curb.

"You are getting sleepy," we say.

"My departure is imminent," he says.

"You are getting sleepy."

"My departure is imminent."

"You are getting sleepy.…"

THE HORIZONTAL BRIGADE

In the old days, the horizontal brigade won every battle. They had weapons causing death more exotic than cobra bites, but they never used them. Their music, played while hiding behind anything horizontal (fallen oaks, divans, abandoned carriages) was their strength. Charmed horses would offer their glittering manes as booty when so tantalized. Foxholes were their dollhouses, and so they were lovingly guarded. It was only in emergencies that they called up the reserves, the infamous ponies, immune to gravity that bombed the clubfoot tanks. Veteran drivers surrendered more out of novelty than fear. Only once, at the famous Battle of the Twirling Mists, were they known to use the ultimate weapon, the costumes that rendered them vertical yet fierce. Today we are surprised that such men could have existed. It is like imagining the Age of Reason, when bearded philosophers drowned in gold bathtubs under the magnetic gaze of admiring disciples.

Utopia TV Store

Amid rows of televisions, screens blank as postcards from cemeteries, we lose ourselves. And while we wait to have our sets repaired, we discuss the owner's inventions: a shadow that never changes length or width, a test pattern of pure memory adapting through the ages of man.

Who says there are no heroes? We love the way he plunges his hand into sets, no regard for personal safety. It's those explosions no more frightening than weather reports from other cities that calm us.

Often customers who die leave their TVs in his care, he told us with some tenderness. "Here's one a widow left behind ten years ago Watching it is like washing clothes underwater. Total immersion. And let me tell you. It's better off than most of us. Inherited a Cadillac Seville, a houseboat, an empty lot in Queens. But does it need anything? Examine its console. Dark, smooth. Look at the antenna. No rigidity there. Relaxed, wanting nothing."

"Of course it's happy here," we add, taking out usual cue. Yes, Utopia TV Store is always open. Even on Christmas Eve we're treated as guests. Mistletoe decking the sets. Perry Como beaming in on every capable tube as we focus our eyes on a pinpoint. Automatically tuning in and fading out, we listen to the steady *click, click,* knowing we owe it our lives, more hazy and blurred with each day.

Maxine Chernoff

THE SHOE AND THE CITY

A woman answers the phone every day saying "Kill me" to the paperboy, "Kill me" to the grocer, the beautician. A man is arrested for the offense of passivity, being quiet in a theater. These things happen in the city, where a judge could be a glass of water. A worn-out shoe bangs itself on a table to make a legal point. But what are they doing in the haberdasher? Burning their coats to believe in the afterlife of their pockets? Burying their dead under piles of shirts to rejuvenate the wretched stripes, the fraying cuffs? And that single footprint in the park—a gift from the road that leads to endless cafés where coffee glistens, a portrait of your own glass heart.

A Sense of Humor

A lion won't attack if you have a sense of humor. Deadly canines become child's colored clay, angry claws, so many handshakes. So you embrace him, careful not to fall from the celluloid cliff that the two of you call home. Before he was a pirate, who could make you walk a transparent plank. Now he is your neighbor, attentive to his topiary garden. Of course this happens in a dream in which an alligator is dashed against an island like a teacup. Of course it is the lion with the real sense of humor. Seeing a woman in a leopard coat, he breaks from his diamond-studded leash. With his paws upon her shoulders, he greets her like a favorite aunt or a college roommate, the practical joker. The woman falls on the ground, her lips a panicky smear. The lion crouches at the curb, a taxi with a broken meter.

Anonymous Thoughts from Home

Sometimes I feel as though I'm walking backwards or live in a forgotten age. After all, aren't we rickety chairs, rattling to prove our worth? And yet in living we can be generous and think a vital thought.

At least that's what I thought. Once on a train going backwards, I met a man too generous for his own good. To flatter me, he guessed my age, and I, to prove him foolish, said, "Sir, I am a chair."

An idea too is a design, the chair on which I sit abstracted. Had I thought myself a genius, trying to prove that one can live a life viewed backwards? No, this is not a comforting age when it is facile to be generous.

Coleridge was not a generous man. He never offered a chair to visitors, even of an advanced age. Still I think of his phrase, "toy of thought," with veneration. "Thought of toy" is the same phrase backwards. (What does that prove?)

Giving gifts may not prove you generous. A socially backward man might give a camera to a blind man. Did you ever offer a chair to a visitor who couldn't sit? I must admit it entered my thought. Try, if you have the inclination, to give a sports car to a mummy despite its age.

When is it said that a philosophy comes of age?
Do primary colors always prove true to their nature?
Can an animal think an unoriginal thought?
Would it be generous to offer a stranger your child?
Who invented the reclining chair?
Will the best man win if he can only walk backwards?

If I could travel backwards to a kinder age, I'd buy a comfortable chair, a document to prove that people once were generous; at least that's what they thought.

Maxine Chernoff

THE WOMAN WHO STRADDLED THE GLOBE

A woman straddles the globe. Her legs, like trees, become rooted in place, one foot on the North Pole, one on the South. The globe, bowing in resignation, is a sullen cowboy whose lasso is a whisper. Her voice rings out, cresting the oceans, one wave at a time. Under the woman the mountains listen to friendly advice. Each day the woman's florid spread grows new bouquets until the things around her (*sorrys, lamplight, breakfasts*), the very things that lovingly called her "Roof," disappear into the hands of forgetfulness.

In the Hospital

I'm in the hospital to have a baby. My two roommates are a porpoise and a tiny woman. The nurses are oblivious to us. One has put at least ten coats of pearl pink polish on her hideously sharp nails. I'm still able to walk around, and because I am in better shape than my two roommates, I find myself assuming the nurse's duties. Every fifteen minutes I must submerge the porpoise's head in a large bowl of water so that she may breathe. When I lift her, her body feels clammy and strange against my white hospital gown. The woman is on the delivery table, legs in stirrups. When I look up her to see if the baby's head is about to crown, I am able to view all of her vital organs in textbook color. Finally I get so aggravated from lack of assistance that I hit the nurse with the porpoise's tail. She keeps polishing her nails.

THE TIME OF THE PLAGUE

It is assumed that bicycles had not been invented in the time of the plague, that doctors trudged from hut to hut carrying leeches and impotent salves. Soon the streets became empty as families succumbed, oblivious as weeds to their communal fate.

Those somehow immune to the plague carried a burden of guilt. Why had they, rather than saintly children survived? The living came to identify with flies, flourishing amid the shambles of generations. They hid their achievements so the plague alone would typify the era.

Historians, noting the lack of invention, called the time of the plague The Dark Ages. Yet today, unearthing villages in remote parts of Europe, it is not unusual to find handlebars, tires, and spokes, buried like ancient reptiles.

The Stand-Up Tragedians

They wear ski masks like thieves, or the white ties of morticians. The lead x-ray apron is common to all, a badge of their calling. Doctors, priests, and the chronically ill make the best tragedians, knowing the division between body and soul to be arbitrary as time itself.

The prevalent one-line tragedians have replaced TV comedians and clowns. "Did you hear the one about the baby who was eaten by a collie?" (Fade out) "Did you know there is a new dread disease discovered every day?" (Fade out).

There is no laughter, no nervous applause. Each person in the audience is still as an opossum playing dead.

At circuses there are children's tragedians, many of whom are ex-teachers and psychiatrists. To the accompaniment of blaring bugles, they shout, "Children, your mommy and daddy are dead!" This simple sentence proves more effective than the hilarious crack of the slapstick to provoke wide-eyed wonder.

The ethnic tragedians charm crowds from Miami to Harlem with tales of the Holocaust and African famine. I even saw one who cleverly used a backdrop of Hitler's baby photo. Poor taste? Hardly. I observed many graying gentlemen thanking him, feeling, to quote one, as if he'd been hit by a bus.

There are a few good women tragedians, but as in all professions, there are obstacles. I know one who dresses like a man and pantomimes ways to get killed in the city. Her backdrop is boarded-up buildings and sometimes she uses real rats. She performs without them in restaurants, however, since too much verisimilitude decreases food sales.

Stand-up tragedians are proud of their art and chide their comedian predecessors for what they call the Sleight-of-Truth Trick. They contend that nothing can be humorous, what with _____, _____, _____, etc. I leave it to you to fill in your favorite calamities and broken promises. No consensus exists, even among the best stand-up tragedians, who call comedians "simians in patent leather shoes." For what is a fright wig compared to a scalping, a fake carnation compared to an artificial limb?

How was it that the stand-up tragedians could have become so much a part of our lives? They're not original and not even thoroughly modern. Who were the prophets? Isn't God a master of the art with his penchant for cheap misery? I think it's the familiarity we love.

In every nightmare they shake our hands, disguised as our innermost fears. They wear clothes that resemble ours but somehow aged fifty years and shrunken. We even try to be like them, affecting a poker face in the supermarket, a muffled voice at family gatherings. Our children understand by now when we say to them, "Sit down. I have some bad news for you." We're only practicing.

New Year's Eve

I'm tired of sloppy drunks thinking my carpet their mother's cozy laps. No more claustrophobic stockbrokers, tight heartbeats trapped next to mine all night. Candlelight dinners are a bore. After the soufflé, his mustache like fly wings, my face an angry clock. This year I'll have the perfect party, intimate gaiety, compact variety, only one guest: the man with twelve personalities.

I met him at the grocery buying ingredients for a Czech, Mexican, Japanese, etc., dinner. His voices are various as parade floats, his glances stylized as poodle haircuts. But tonight he's promised no tricks. Dreamy Fred will gladly mix the punch, lumps of sherbet dripping like old magnolia blossoms. John will pass out party hats, selfish John—Napoleon one moment, Sherlock Holmes the next, he leaves me on my own.

And what are parties without the hors d'oeuvres, tray upon tray like colored buttons? "A deviled egg, Charles?" Charles abstracted, Charles the studious, squints up as if the room were a foggy landscape.

"Some herring paté, Eric?" Eric the sulker, gazing at the ground, one foot on the carpet, one yearning toward the ledge sighs, "No."

Meanwhile, you wonder, where are the others? Joe, Richard, and Martin late as usual. Dan, ill in bed (his migraines), and Bob, never much for parties, listens to everything just outside the door. We mustn't embarrass him.

At 11:45, Al, who has gone to get more ice, returns. His hands are cold. And just when champagne is to be uncorked, just when noisemakers are to unfurl their tasteless flags and confetti fill the room like some exotic virus, William passes out, drunk again. "Should have left him off the list," I mutter. "We'll lay him on the bed. I'll move the coat."

Maxine Chernoff

Midnight, deep bass snoring. Guy Lombardo playing "Auld Lang Syne." "Cheers," I say to the refrigerator.

FROM *NEW FACES OF 1952* (1985)

Lost and Found

I am looking for the photo that would make all the difference in my life. It's very small and subject to fits of amnesia, turning up in poker hands, grocery carts, under the unturned stone. The photo shows me at the lost and found looking for an earlier photo, one that would have made all the difference then. My past evades me like a politician. Wielding a flyswatter, it destroys my collection of cereal boxes, my childhood lived close to the breakfast table. Only that photo can help me locate my fourteen lost children, who look just like me. When I call the Bureau of Missing Persons, they say, "Try the Bureau of Missing Photos." They have a fine collection. Here's one of Calvin Coolidge's seventh wedding. Here's one of a man going over a cliff on a dogsled. Here's my Uncle Arthur the night he bought the prize peacock. Oh, photo! End your tour of the world in a hot-air balloon. Resign your job at the mirror-testing laboratory. Come home to me, you little fool, before I find I can live without you.

BIOGRAPHIA LITERARIA

You remember *New Faces of 1952*, entertainers blurred and green as bad counterfeit. From her lap you watched your mother watch TV. Sometimes she'd accompany the aquamarine vocalist in *Sentimental Journey*, but always during commercials she looked confused. Was she trying to separate your squalling from your future as critics detach art from art? The dominant hue was infant red. Face it. Your childhood was shaped by daily viewing of *Divorce Court*. To enhance your witness-box approach to life, you began each sentence with "Your Honor" and practiced crying in a full-length mirror. As credits cascaded down the screen, you admired the boomers and gaffers, unheralded as bacteria. By now your tears had a charisma so strong they performed without you at Edsel sales. With the crisp, high step of majorettes, they preceded you down Main Street. When your mother questioned, you pleaded the Fifth or practiced evasion: "Inventing the enemy," you said in the mirror. An optimist, she labeled you artistic. The other choice was worse.

The Smell Convention

Like a zoo with only one animal, like a doctor who listens to hearts through a yam, I was a rarity. What was I doing at the smell convention? But I had a civic duty. Who else might testify against lemons, those prissy pouters? Who else might nix nectarines? My sense of smell, acute as bats' radar, was my credential. I wore it on my face like a tear in a flag. I was after the riot of smells that engulfs us in stores, circuses, our own sad bodies. If there were only one smell to cope with, bland as a nurse, we would be free.

"You can't go on like that," I told the delegate from Utah, who was spraying himself with essence of the Great Salt Lake.
"Death to dogwood!" I interrupted the keynote speaker, whose garlic necklace was studded with cough drops.

Oh, they were subtle! Overcome by elixir of Reuben sandwich, I staggered to my chair. It smelled of last week's rainstorm on the eleventh green. Where could I hide? Tiny smell arrows were everywhere.

Trying to remain calm, I slipped on my wetsuit and dove in. I swam in a sea of Girl Scout cookies, dripping batteries, *eau de* key-in-the-lock, sailors' bed sheets.

Spring

Mrs. Smith takes Mr. Smith in the closet while the children dream in unison of Napoleon. It happens every spring. Spirit pounds flesh, and you think the newsman said 'languor.' Next door the professor is vibrantly thinking, theories brightening the room at 9 p.m. *So,* he sighs, *in this instance the British spelling is correct.* A fruit fly circles over his dictionary. Another battle won. In the nearby church a bell insists in the highest tower. It reminds us of a toothache or nostalgia. Meanwhile, she's ripped her nylons on his limitations. He wears suspenders, the nerve! You close your eyes and point to a map, finding yourself in an Amazon so blue you worry for the ocean. That's the give and the take of it, the getting out of yourself at least for a stroll down the Avenue of Busted Cups. It's March 19th, time to slaughter the poinsettia. A white milk oozes from the stem onto the mahogany. The king is dead. If your ideas had form, like a milk bottle left on the porch, you'd take them in the closet and caress them. You wouldn't be discreet. You'd understand the implications but finally wouldn't care. After all, this is a poem about love.

Prophecy

I read to improve myself: *The Sensible Cheerleader, Diseases of Guinea Fowl,* or a Russian romance in whose names I drown. Pyulashkin weds Livertoveska despite the complaints of Federovich and the czar. Oh, for the simplicity of a house at midnight! Oh, for the modest lines of a cracked plate. Pressing a giant poppy between two limp pages, I grow tired. I run my fingers over words thick as shrubbery. On a fresh sheet of paper I write line after line, gray smudges like an aerial view of refugees winding through tundra. The lines between the writing form the words: "Once a woman grew so weary that she died of reading."

A Name

Suppose your parents had called you Dirk. Wouldn't that be motive enough to commit a heinous crime, just as Judies always become nurses and Brads, florists? After the act, your mom would say, "He was always a good boy. Once on my birthday, he gave me one of those roses stuck in a glass ball. You know; the kind that never gets soggy"— her Exhibit A. Exhibit B: a surprised corpse, sharing a last name of Dirk with the mortician. And Dad would say, "Dirk once won a contest by spelling the word 'pyrrhic,'" and in his alcohol dream he sees the infant Dirk signing his birth certificate with a knife. Still, Dirk should have known better. He could tell you that antimony is Panama's most important product. He remembered Vasco de Gama and wished him well. Once he'd made a diorama of the all-American boyhood: a little farm, cows the size of nails, cotton-ball sheep, a corncob silo, but when he signed it Dirk, the crops were blighted by bad faith. And don't forget Exhibits C, D, E. The stolen éclair, the zoo caper, the taunting of a certain Miss W, who smelled of fried onions. It was his parents' fault. They called him Dirk.

Identity Principle

Triplets are so embarrassing, too much soup in the soup of life. Who needs an alphabet with three *O*s, a tangled birth, a troika of woes? Picture the mother swelled as a cloud, the gallop of three heartbeats like a posse through her. Or twins, those clever monkeys, allowed to eat at table. Identical birthmarks, matching hairnets, the sound and the echo. And old age: one twin wheels the other before him, meeting himself after the stroke. So you decide even among brothers and sisters raucous as wedding guests, to be an only child. The stance you take in making love, in walking crookedly, in robbing the sperm bank. Until you have a child and people say, "She looks just like you." In her face you see the same wish to be an island so distant she'll never see another pleasure boat.

SOTTO VOCE

Although she's only four, my daughter knows Spanish. Say *Blanco,* she demands, say *Negro.* Words are the finest toys, she tells me with eyes that are arrows. My husband speaks with the virtuosity of a drummer: *suspiration, humidor, revivify.* Beautiful words float upwards like jets sewing clouds. If my cat could only speak, it would be in shrill, nasal French I wouldn't understand. Languages wash over me, scratched on cold telephone booths, tapped on windowpanes. I am sorry to admit that I am inventing yet another, in the dark, furtively as one imagines an obscene old kiss. Just as I am thinking about it, my daughter shouts, *Verde, Verde.* She thinks so much depends on it—palm trees, parsley, dollar bills—that I can't disappoint her. *Foolish girl,* I think, locking up my new language. Then *Verde* dissolves, naked and bloodless, into the busy air.

Sayings of my Distant Uncle

for Henry Gordon

Every family has one, the genius who cheats at poker, the living myth. Once, on *You Bet Your Life,* he outdistanced the duck on the screen with his good, uncommon sense. Sometimes our father would sit us on his knee and take out the family photo to which my uncle's profile had been glued; grainy, gray, looking the other way. Rumors were he was a tuba player, a lumberjack, a rabbi. He lived in Dallas, Nairobi, Buffalo Falls. Married to Shirley, Esther, Dot, and Queenie. (We liked to imagine the last one a beautiful collie.) Mother hated when he was mentioned, whistling through our senses like a curveball. And sometimes there'd be letters whisked off to drawers. Among my father's rubbers, souvenir photos of swordfish, Navy shrapnel, we'd open them. My sister read, "If you are unconscious, don't let it show." I liked, "The only thing I trust in life is bad art."

Miss Congeniality

Even as an embryo, she made room for "the other guy." Slick and bloody, she emerged quietly. Why spoil the doctor's best moment? When Dad ran over her tricycle, she curtsied, and when Mom drowned her kittens, she smiled, a Swiss statuette. Her teachers liked the way she sat at her desk, composed as yesterday's news. In high school she decorated her locker with heart-shaped doilies and only went so far, a cartoon kiss at the door. She read the classics, *The Glamorous Dolly Madison,* and dreamed of marrying the boy in the choir whose voice never changed. Wedding photos reveal a waterfall where her face should be. Her husband admired how she bound her feet to buff the linoleum. When she got old, she remembered to say pardon to the children she no longer recognized, smiling sons and daughters who sat at her bedside watching her fade to a wink.

Hairdo

Part avalanche, part retort, it begins inside the unknowing scalp. Pay attention to the symptoms. No matter how even the part, how tight the bun, a hairdo may take residence. Squatters' rights exist outside the law: try arresting a hairdo. The compelling insistence of the hairdo to a life of its own (witness its growth after death) rivals the legendary tenacity of gold prospectors. The day it is born the will collapses. The mind embraces the change like a convert a picture of his prophet.

It is Tuesday. And the fern that is her hairdo has grown overnight. First she is logical—what did she eat for dinner? what dream? The comb is useless and so is the scarf. So she boards the usual bus for work, beaming randomly at passengers, thankful for their discretion. Not only do they ignore her fern but the nun with the shopping bag bangs and the driver with the broccoli coif. (Strange she never noticed them before.) Or is it that only she can detect the change, as the adolescent girl in her dark bedroom touches her breasts, growing like radishes under the skin?

Maxine Chernoff

Learning to Listen

When I was eight, I got the measles. For two weeks, my parents like to recall, I was sick as sin, sick as a dog, sick as a scurvied sailor. My fever over one hundred three degrees, I lay in bed remembering odd parcels of language: *Children should be seen and not spoil the soup. Phil, fix the helicopter so it won't snow on our layer cake.* Sleep offered no relief. My mind spun with mythological half-breeds, dachshunds welded to Airedales, my friend Ginny joined at the waist to a telephone pole. Trying to describe my visions to my worried parents, I was offered a camphored towel.

After a week of semi-consciousness, I came around. Smelling like a new person, I sat up in bed and demanded entertainment. Since my eyes were light-sensitive, my mother suggested I listen to records I'd never heard, ballads about golf, Coney Island, and kreplach, containing bawdy metaphors I didn't then understand. I had been so ill that time was no longer a continuum of experience. Listening to Lenny and the Jewish Rednecks was my childhood. Even after the illness passed and the records were stashed, whenever my mother spoke, I still heard, *Parsnip, if you don't take out the zero factor, you won't get your declension this week.*

Animal Magnetism

Even among skeptics, Mesmer's garden is the talk of Vienna. On any given day, one can observe delighted citizens strolling down rows of real horses standing still as shrubs or reclining on pigs tastefully transformed into loveseats. Sometimes after it rains on the sheep picnic tables, honeymooners have their portraits painted against the whitest possible background. If the painter is talented, he can capture the rainbow growing out of the bed of chameleons. In the night local children sometimes damage the landscape. Mesmer says it is not malice but the spirit of scientific discovery that prompts them to pluck the rose-covered chicken arbor. During the monthly séances for those sick of spirit, bodies float lightly over the pig loveseats. Others awaiting their cure discern in these clouds the trembling only they desire.

Maxine Chernoff

How We Went

It used to be we'd die of grippe, malodorous breath, or by a curse. Death was generic, like the peas I bought yesterday, smaller, but, yes, pea-green. Some by an oversight, the heart an erratic drummer, or by an obsession, a thought ice-fast in brain. Observed without explanation: the sinking of a steeple through an attic window, the sudden dimming of one's shoes, a slackening of hatred for a friend. Suppose a man said good-night to his wife and by some sign she knew: a kettle belched, a cat arched under a chair, or her own breath caught like a faulty clock-hand.

Anger

The hit parade: "I Left my Anger in San Francisco, Wichita, Boise, and Beloit." Shoppers demanding as dental drills, infants raging like saints. The professor assigns the history of the toe in 750 words. Puzzled, the student strokes her chin, pitted as the moon, leftover anger lighting the sky at eight a.m. Salt, the aftertaste, ammonia, the smell of our best perfume. The winning poet reads, "On the Anger of Balding in Venice While on a Grant." Yes, the audience is huge with anger and reads chairs. Anger the cause: a phone slammed down. Anger the effect: a hand bruised on a plum. Our highest art: the anger of machines; the razor's gotten out of hand. Anger, the ticklish executioner, waves to us from a train, and while the blizzard rages outside, anger brings the buzzards home to Hinckley, Ohio, every March fifteenth. I heard it on the news.

Maxine Chernoff

THE EDIBLE HARP

I couldn't play it. No, I couldn't play it. All those years the majestic instrument stood at my bedside. Like an arthritic butler, it was the first thing that saluted me in the morning, dignified, useless. I teased it with symphonies. I sang an aria into its huge waiting ear. Poor Aunt Perdita never expected such misery to come of her gift. I imagined her a corpulent angel, waiting to hear a better result. But when I tried to play the harp, coconuts rolled onto a marble floor,
mine shafts echoed with disaster, roosters fought in barnyards, and police chiefs mated.

Distracted one evening, I found myself nibbling some wood from its elegant frame. A few days later I tried gnawing a string. Yes, I heard music—air, vacancy, pure thought.

Beginning, Middle, End

It happened in the Azores without much fanfare. They appeared in *Vanity Fair* as the floodlit, tan couple, faces down in the sand. She was horsy. He was thought-bound. They read the *Times* at breakfast, love inspiring them to finish the crossword puzzle by noon. She was vertical; he was horizontal. Then the dark road, the row of pink houses glowing from the inside like jack-o'-lanterns at midnight. Who could have guessed he'd be so changed by a notion one-sided as moss or that she'd see him as a hamper brimming with mismatched ideas? It ended, and they forgot each other as children do dead milkmen, as widowers forget the pears left to ripen on the windowsill.

THE UNZIPPED

In times of boxer shorts depicting steeplechases, we envy the unzipped. Listen, I'm talking to you, children with milk in your mouths and widows who sleep with their clothes on in case of fire. The unzipped are among us. If you ask them their dreams, they say *the man who invented swimming* or merely *castanets.* You may have spoken to one of them in the drugstore this morning, that sweaty young man, shameless as the weather. Dare I send you reeling like a migraine? You, stranger, might be married to one. To find out, perform this test. Check into a lousy hotel whose neon has shrunk to a twitch. Tell your husband you're going out for a sandwich but return five minutes later. Does he stare at you with the reluctance of a bootblack? Or observe. Does he worship lizards, his nonchalant cousins? Does he lose buttons as regularly as you receive junk mail?

And what of the burden on the zipped, those commuter train jockeys, those flat-on-the-back sleepers. Isn't it unfair how the unzipped always get away with things? Your sister was one with her slippery childhood, those children who shouted in movies, the pretty teacher who laughed at the jokes of the worst student. Face it: only you are zipped.

FROM *LEAP YEAR DAY: NEW AND SELECTED POEMS* (1990)

How Lies Grow

The first time I lied to my baby, I told him it was his face on the baby-food jar. The second time I lied to my baby, I told him that he was the best baby in the world, that I hoped he'd never leave me. Of course I want him to leave me someday. I don't want him to become one of those fat shadows who live in their mother's houses watching game shows all day. The third time I lied to my baby, I said, "Isn't she nice?" of the old woman who'd caressed him in his carriage. She was old and ugly and had a disease. The fourth time I lied to my baby, I told him the truth, I thought. I told him how he'd have to leave me someday or risk becoming a man in a bow-tie who eats macaroni on Fridays. I told him it was for the best, but then I thought, *I want him to live with me forever. Someday he'll leave me. Then what will I do?*

THE APOLOGY STORE

I needed an all-purpose apology for the many occasions I had surely forgotten and was to forget. It could be vague and unshaped as the future or distinct as a map of the ancestral country printed in Braille. My funds were unlimited, my purpose a banner of good intentions.

"We're sorry, "they said, but currency won't do.

"I have small bills and large," I offered.

"American or foreign currencies aren't accepted. We're sorry."

"Then charge one of each and gift-wrap them, please." Even if I staggered under a pile tall as Jacob's ladder, I'd get them to the car."

"Our spring line is sold out, and our summer line is threatened by numerous strikes. It's touch and go, and I'm ..."

"Sorry," I finished, a little short of my usual good cheer. "Perhaps I can leave my name. You can call me when a few arrive."

"What with strikes by anchor-forgers, spinach-choppers, and midwives ..."

"I can understand your problems, and I'm sorry you're having them." The clerk bore an uncanny resemblance to my grandfather, so I decided to appeal on family lines. I shed a single, theatrical tear. I waved my arms like a *Perpetuum Mobile* at a departure gate. The clerk remained silent.

Down on my knees, I asked for a promise, "Will you call me when your supply is shipped?"

Now he looked like the yellow cocker spaniel I'd lost on a Sunday picnic forty years ago.

"I'm sorry," he said. "We don't have a phone."

Maxine Chernoff

The New Money

for K. G. E.

Ones: white for purity. A white man says his prayers in a white room. White nightshirt. White hair. In the background (raised velveteen relief) is an altar. Impaled on a stalagmite: the old money. "Self-reference is our motto" is reflected in a real mirror shaped like the continental forty-eight. Squint and you can see the Rockies. Cost: $49.98, discounted for summer white sale.

Fives: Colossal black olives rest on a bed of generals and wanted men, who appear agitated, anonymous as canned goods. They are the first designer bills with Salvador Dali's signature in gold leaf. There's a run on the Chase Manhattan as they are bought up by counter-agents trying to strengthen the zloty. They are duplicated by forgers in developing nations where unemployed PhDs are used as cheap labor. Finally replaced by Norman Rockwell money, familiar and comfortable. Nobody wants to steal it.

Tens: out of circulation. Fear of decimals in high places. The president sleeps with mittens and wingtips. What more can be said of the intimate nature of currency?

Thirteens: largest of bills. Featuring football fields, battleships named after women in the thirties, hair fetishes, arenas where flamenco dancers practice voluntary metabolism. Reverse side: an appeal to sentiment. Paw raised in a friendly salute, everyone's favorite pet is quoted (in Latin) as saying, "I am snowing on your capital, a lost Caravaggio, a taxidermist's dream of islands in relief."

FROM *WORLD: POEMS 1991–2001*
(2001)

Nomads

Since I've left Chicago, I always worry about my mother's plans for Thanksgiving. It's not that she can't join me out here—she can if she'd like—but she rarely feels up to traveling. There aren't major illnesses in the way, but her own habit of reclusiveness. This year, I'm happy but somewhat surprised to hear that her bus driver has invited my mother over for Thanksgiving dinner. He's not just any bus driver, she tells me, but a nice man named Ray. She'll be a guest along with the bus driver's girlfriend, who is sixty but looks forty, and her two grandchildren. I tell her to bring something to dinner. This is knowledge that an eighty-year-old woman should possess but somehow my mother may have missed in life. I can't remember my parents ever having had friends. I thought that friendships stopped at some exact age and spent my early thirties wondering when friends were going to desert me. When they didn't I became peevish to test their loyalty. I tell my mother to bring wine. She wonders where she will get it. I tell her that Walgreen's has a decent selection, knowing that it's in the course of her limited travels. She wonders if she should bring Manischevitz. I tell her that only she likes sweet wine and that her bus driver probably isn't Jewish. Even when she was younger, my mother would add sugar to wine, even to champagne. I tell her to buy a Chardonnay, but I can tell she is losing interest. Maybe she should bring something for the children, she says. What children? The nice lady's grandchildren. The girlfriend. She's smarter than he is, my mother adds. Almost passed her CPA exam three times. This impresses my mother, whose husband was a CPA. Maybe you can bring them chocolate turkeys or snowmen, I suggest. In Chicago, seasons are a cold or hot blur. Thanksgiving and Christmas are interchangeable, as are their icons. Leaves are gone from trees, the world barely alive by early November. Turkeys or *nomads?* she asks. Where will I find chocolate nomads? S-n-o-w-m-e-n, I spell. What? S-n-o-w-m-e-n. Snowmen, she says softly, as if our conversation is making her run out of breath.

Beauty

Men are beautiful. This is something we usually don't admit. Maybe we've given up on claiming beauty for our side.

We've ceded the territory to men who've cooked up industries to harvest beauty: fashion, plastic surgery, pornography, to name a few.

That's why death becomes so important. It reconnects us to our original claim.

Her son asks, "Would you care if he weren't so gorgeous?"

Her son can see the dead man's beauty because he isn't a man yet. He hasn't become a specialist or entrepreneur.

When he sees a gorgeous man, he knows that women are right.

The gorgeous man was famous for being the son of a gorgeous man. The newsman has stated that he wasn't extraordinarily bright or talented, which puzzles her son. Why is his mother spending his weekend in tears? Would she cry like this if he hadn't a fine nose, a sensitive brow, deep lively eyes?

What if he looked like a pig, her son asks.

She tries to be honest. If he looked like a pig, she probably wouldn't cry unless she knew him.

How can she explain that her display is a ritual involving hope?

We cry when we lose hope, she suggests to her son.

You didn't lose your hope, her son replies.

He's angry at her and won't admit, though he's beginning to understand, the high price we pay for this loan.

Heavenly Bodies

—When is that huge meteor scheduled to hit Earth?

—I heard something about 2035.

—You mean in thirty-seven years the world might end?

—The world wouldn't end.

—If a meteor of that size hits Earth, we'll be destroyed.

—We might be destroyed, but there'd still be a world.

—Do you mean a universe?

—I guess that's what I mean.

—How will there be a universe if we're not there to form the concept?

—Do you think we're so important that the whole universe can't exist if we don't? What was here before we were born?

—History was here.

—That's exactly it. We're simply a part of it all, like a whorl in a tree trunk.

—Why didn't you say a grain of sand on a beach?

—Okay, a grain of sand on a beach.

—How can someone who knows so much about the universe be persuaded to use a cliché?

—Death is a cliché.

—What do you mean?

—It's given to us, and we can do nothing to change it.

—But you're saying our own deaths don't matter. Not now. Not in thirty-seven years, not if the universe gets destroyed.

—Exactly.

—So what should we do?

—About what?

—What should we do to prevent the meteor from destroying us?

—I guess we could intercept it.

—Who, you and me?

—The government.

—I knew it.

—Knew what?

—You're some kind of hired assassin.

—What do you mean?

—You're hired by the government to make me think I don't matter, not even if I die.

—How does that make me an assassin?

—It's conceptual. You erase me with your thoughts.

—So maybe I'm more of an artist than an assassin.

—How much do they pay you?

—Who?

—The government.

—Why would the government hire me to convince you of anything? Is either of us so important?

—Here you go again. You just won't admit it.

—Admit what?

—That when we die the universe will perish.

—Okay. When we die the universe will perish. Does that make you feel better?

—Yes, momentarily.

Wearing Moe

—What's that on your shoulder?

—A tattoo.

—A tattoo of what?

—A Celtic emblem.

—When did you get it?

—When I was in college.

—What does it mean?

—I don't know.

—Did you used to know?

—I never knew what it meant.

—But what if it means something terrible?

—Like what?

—Well, maybe it says, "Kill the Jews!" or "Reagan in 1980," or "If guns are outlawed, only outlaws will have guns."

—Did the Celts have guns?

—I'm just saying it might mean something bad.

—Well, even if it were bad, it wouldn't be bad to me because I don't know it. Besides, it was one of his best choices.

—What were the others?

—Moe or a butterfly.

—Moe?

—You know, Moe of the Three Stooges.

—You mean the tattoo artist only did three tattoos?

—He wasn't certified yet. He was just learning. Besides, I thought this one was pretty.

—Aren't butterflies pretty?

—Not the one he had.

—No?

—It looked like labia.

—Maybe it was labia.

—He said it was a butterfly.

—And you never asked what your tattoo meant?

—That's right. Or I don't remember. I was pretty drunk when I did this.

—Did you go alone?

—No, my old boyfriend went with me. He got Moe on his forearm.

—Where is he now?

—Where is Moe?

—Where is the boyfriend?

—He's a grade-school principal in Georgia.

—With Moe on his forearm?

—He probably wears long sleeves.

Her Many Occupations

—All these years I've been writing novels, I've felt like an elephant trainer.

—Why an elephant?

—The ideas just sit there, heavy and still, and you have to make them work.

—And why is that like training an elephant?

—An elephant isn't exactly pliable.

—How does it feel when you write other things?

—After writing novels, writing anything else makes me feel like I'm running a flea circus.

—So you prefer elephants to fleas?

—I didn't say that.

—Well, do you?

—Both are dangerous work.

—Why dangerous?

—Because poems and stories are invisible, and novels so formidable.

—So why not just quit writing?

—I couldn't do that. I'd have no purpose.

—But writing sounds like it makes you so unhappy, so put-upon.

—I didn't mean to suggest that. I was just trying out metaphors for this new piece.

—What is this new writing?

—An essay.

—And what animal-handling is essay-writing comparable to?

—It's like arranging flowers for a still-life.

—Flowers aren't animals.

—That's true.

Guilt

—I saw a bumper sticker that said, "I'm trying to become the person that my dog thinks I am."

—What does that mean?

—You know how dogs think the best of you?

—They're loyal.

—Loyal and true.

—We should probably get a dog.

—But they're so needy.

—They want to have something to do with you. Is that a problem?

—Even when you're not interested, they're panting in your face.

—Isn't that comforting? A pet that actually needs you?

—They have those sad brown eyes.

—They gaze at you with adoration.

—They remind me of old people.

—Why old people?

—Your grandma's in a rest home and you visit for an hour. And when you try to leave, she stands by the exit and stares at you, sadly, like a dog.

—So you don't want to own a dog because it reminds you of your grandmother?

—Only my grandmother had blue eyes.

—Then we should get a husky.

—Why a husky?

—Huskies have blue eyes.

—Aren't huskies part wolf?

—Aren't humans part primate?

—If you're trying to tell me that you want to adopt a chimpanzee, I'd rather have a dog.

HUSBAND AND WIFE

—I'm a bad mother.

—Were you a bad daughter before you were a bad mother?

—Not necessarily.

—Then how did you learn to be a bad mother?

—It was my children, their particular issues, and my own troubles as a person.

—As a person, not a mother?

—I'm also a writer, a teacher, and a wife.

—So what are your troubles as a writer, a teacher, and a wife?

—I don't have many. Mainly as a wife, teacher, and writer, I'm worried about being a bad mother.

—And what do you do that makes you a bad mother?

—I never bake cookies.

—Is that all?

—I don't got to PTA suppers

—Is that all?

—I tell my children the truth about things.

—Give me an example.

—A daughter will ask if she should be a cheerleader, and I tell her she shouldn't.

—Why shouldn't she?

—I don't think girls should stand on the sidelines and cheer while boys do things.

—Don't cheerleaders cheer for women's sports as well?

—Maybe they do. See what I mean?

—What do you mean?

—Life is too full. You can't know all the interpretations, so you end up a bad mother by accident as well as on purpose.

—You're a bad mother on purpose?

—No. Who said that?

—I think you did.

—Who are you to judge me? Are you someone's mother?

—No, I'm your child's father.

—Then you know the answers already. Why are you asking me?

—So I can see why you think you're a bad mother.

—Do you think I'm a bad mother?

—No worse than I am a father.

—You're a good father.

—Then you must be a good mother.

— That is, usually.

—I'm only usually a good father?

—Sometimes you're not so good.

—Like when?

—Like when the boys want help on something and you tell them a long story.

—Narratives provide lessons.

—The boys get impatient. They don't see the point.

—Well, if you were a better mother, they'd see the point.

—So our sons' impatience with your stories proves that I'm a bad mother? Maybe you're a bad storyteller.

—I don't think so.

—What's your proof?

—You like my stories.

—Or I pretend I do.

—That's why you're a good wife even if you're a bad mother.

—Thank you.

—You're welcome.

An Epiphany

—I had an epiphany today at the beauty shop.

—An epiphany about hair?

—An epiphany about attraction.

—What was Clifford doing to you?

—He wasn't doing anything. This young couple, a haircutter and her boyfriend, were having an argument. They were very attractive people, especially him.

—And they were arguing in the store?

—Yes.

—What about?

—About nothing.

—And that was your epiphany?

—No, it wasn't. My epiphany was about how they were touching.

—What do you mean?

—Even though they were arguing, there was sexual energy to it.

—And?

—I thought about us.

—What did you think?

—I though of how terribly we get along.

—That was your epiphany?

—No, I thought how we were like that couple. No matter what's wrong, I'm attracted to you.

—That was your epiphany? We've been together forever, and you just realized you're attracted to me?

—I've always realized it. That was my epiphany.

—So if I become real shabby-looking, it'll be all over for us?

—I don't think so.

—And why is that?

—Because I'll remember what I realized in the beauty shop.

—And you'll still love me?

—This isn't about love. It's about attraction.

Killing Himself

—I feel much better now that my friend isn't going to kill himself.

—Your friend was going to kill himself? How did you know that?

—He talked about it all the time.

—Didn't you send him to a doctor?

—Of course I did.

—And what did the doctor do?

—I'm not quite sure.

—But your friend isn't going to kill himself anymore?

—I don't think so.

—And why was he going to begin with?

—He just felt like it.

—And the doctor changed how he felt?

—Maybe.

—And how did the doctor do that?

—I don't know.

—So what have you learned from this?

—That when people say they're going to kill themselves, either they do or they don't.

—And what if your friend had killed himself?

—I would have changed doctors.

—And if he says it again later?

—Then I'll have him see a doctor again.

—The same doctor?

—Any doctor.

—Oh.

The Method

—If I have twins, I'll name them Medusa and Circe.

—And what if your twins are boys?

—I won't have boys.

—What do you mean you won't have boys?

—I want a girl.

—But women have boys all the time.

—I'm having a baby girl.

—But you can't be sure of that. You get what you get.

—I'm using a method.

—What kind of method?

—You have sex during ovulation to have a girl and sex before ovulation to have a boy.

—Why does that work?

—It has something to do with the sperm's mobility, but maybe I'm getting it wrong. Maybe you have sex before ovulation to get the girl.

—Didn't you say that already?

—Maybe. I can't remember.

—If you can't get the method straight, how are you going to use it?

—I have a book at home. A lady in Massachusetts invented the method.

—Do you have to have sex in Massachusetts?

—It works anywhere. It's ninety percent accurate.

—The other ten percent are boys?

—The other ten percent are whatever the person doesn't want.

—And then what?

—And then what?

—And then what do you do?

—I guess you try again next time.

—But what do you do with the baby?

—What baby?

—The one you've had who's the wrong sex.

—I don't know. Maybe you give it away.

—To that lady.

—What lady?

—The one in Massachusetts whose method you used and failed with.

—Why would she want my baby?

—She wouldn't. I'm kidding.

—This is a serious matter. It's about who lives and who dies.

—I am serious. Here's a baby you don't want. It's wearing a blue blanket. Its name is Jeff. Now what are you going to do with Jeff?

—I'm going to give him to you.

—Why would I want your baby?

—You've expressed concern, so if it's a boy, you can have him.

—But I'm not married. I don't even have a girlfriend.

—Well, congratulations anyway. You're the father of a boy. I think you named him Jeff.

—What about his real father?

—He doesn't have a father.

—How can that be?

—I'm getting inseminated at a clinic.

—Well, maybe the clinic will want the baby. You know, potential customers can see what kind of baby they can expect. The way they display food at Japanese restaurants.

—That's silly.

—Then who's going to take Jeff?

—I'm giving him to you. We're pretty good friends, at work at least.

The Sound

—I hate it when we have sex and you make that sound.

—What sound?

—The sound you make when you're about to have orgasm.

—What sound do you mean?

—I can't describe it. It sounds like no other sound you ever make.

—But why do you hate it?

—It scares me.

—Why would it scare you?

—I guess it's because we're at an intimate moment, and you make an unfamiliar sound.

—It must be my intimate-moment sound.

—But it doesn't sound intimate. It sounds … well … brutal.

—I make a brutal sound?

—Yes, I think that's how I'd describe it.

—Make the sound for me.

—I can't.

—Of course you can. You remember it, don't you?

—I'm embarrassed to make it.

—You're not embarrassed to tell me, but you're embarrassed to make it?

—Right.

—Just try.

—All right. It's something like "Yowwwww-oh-woe-woe."

—And that sounds brutal to you?

—It does.

—It sounds to me like I'm very happy.

—It doesn't sound happy to me.

—What sound would you like me to make?

—I don't have an alternative in mind. I just thought I'd tell you that the sound you make, well, it brings me out of the moment. Sex ends for me when I hear that sound.

—That's good, isn't it?

—Why is it good?

—Because you know I've had an orgasm when you hear it.

—But what if I want to do something more to you?

—More? We've both finished by then. What more would we do?

—What if I still want to kiss you and you're making that sound?

—Well, I guess you could try and see.

—Should I try now?

—Why do you think I want you to kiss me when you can't stand the sound I make at my most vulnerable moment?

—I didn't mean I couldn't stand it. I just meant it's distracting.

—Maybe you should gag me.

—Then you'd make the sound but it would be even worse.

—Why would it be worse?

—It would sound all muffled and sad, like the voice of someone locked inside of a car trunk.

—So you'd rather I sound brutal than all muffled and sad?

—I guess so.

—You must really love me, then.

WASH

A problem of theology: how to wash the hair shirt.

It is the wash that drinks and gets drunk.

She mistook a laundry bag on the road for a white dog.

The silent-film star does her wash in a basement as dark as a crypt.

There are clotheslines where the wash of centuries huddles like immigrants.

Nietzsche did not do his own ironing.

You will never marry if it rains on your wash.

On the cruise he dreamed of pastels.

The flag of servility, a dirty apron.

Women with triangular faces do their wash on the banks of a straight line.

Frozen wash portends the death of a neighbor.

Closely related to voodoo is the missing sock of middle age.

When angels pass you on the street they are embarrassed: their freshly washed wings protrude from their clothes.

Evolution of the Bridge:
from Uncollected Prose Poems

Five Possible Moments

Night Thoughts

It's three in the morning, and the baby is crying again. His wife insists that ten month-olds should be able to calm themselves. She's read a book about it. Why can't he believe her? Lying next to him, she's breathing so softly that it's hard to tell she's alive. Whenever he informs her that Alex woke up in the middle of the night, she simply says, "I didn't hear him." He feels as if he's having an affair with his baby and wants to disclose it, but she won't allow it.

The Heimlich Maneuver

She is a spinner of precise little tales about eating dim sum with one's old boyfriend during a snowstorm on the day that John Lennon is shot. Seated at lunch next to America's top story critic (according to one journal), she is holding her book on her lap. "I want to give you 'The Traffic on Mars,'" she rehearses to herself.

"Pass the potatoes," the famous critic says, "and butter." He is silent throughout lunch. A handsome man, his eating habits make him less so.

She imagines the story she'll write about lunch with the famous critic.

A Valentine

Mario loves Miss Betty Spice more than he thinks imaginable. She is tall and young and pretty, more luscious than his own mother, who doesn't smell so good now that the baby's in the house. He can't wait till Valentine's Day to pin a heart right on her nipple.

Loving a Short Man

When Sheena sees Greta with Maurice, she snickers. How could she have loved him? Standing in line for the movie, Maurice's eyebrows meet Greta's chin. Suddenly she feels insulted for Maurice that Greta is probably noticing that right now. Why are tall women so arrogant?

Simple Gifts

Judy thanked Fred for the Chinese willow laundry basket though she actually hated it. It was smug of him to give her a gift that put her in her place. It was especially odd to receive it on the evening this was to become, as the story assigned him a motive and her a fate.

Origin

Cloudy as a picture of a relative so distant I must squint to see him on the pea-colored photo: Manchuria, 1908. And oh, the train ride The steppes so beautiful in spring with reindeer dancing *pas de deux*. The European bittern making fence repairs with its hammer head. Caviar in cut glass bowls. The Yellow Sea so blue it must have been named by jaundiced men. Iron mines springing up everywhere like hot-dog stands. I'll make the Ural Mountains my coat of arms. Under white exploding stars, I'll find my ancient cousins playing dominoes. I'll sleep on raspberry seats, the shiny steel tracks receding under me like childhood.

A dream of a train so small my window is a postage stamp. Through the Manchurian countryside, I watch the stars fade out one by one, metal ducks in a carnival shooting arcade.

Maxine Chernoff

The Commonplace

The mountain, stiff as a pencil, wanted to rest as a matter of conformity. The king had decreed that all laundry be hung, that the horse, sentenced to death, was to have one wish and one wish only, a rocking chair. Long ago another chair had eloped with a nylon. Long ago children had sprung from the union of a fish and a bullet. But that was before the age of the commonplace, decreed by the new king. As a form of revolt, a dead man demanded a new silk fedora. Remembering the past, the calendar tried to shoot down a cloud. "The Flag of the Commonplace," they called it, when I swung perpendicular from a flagpole, my legs flapping, my chest, stars.

Quizzing Glass

Too much telepathy swirls in the air-locked land. We've divined the future as mystics in South Carolina see cream on a porch in Vermont. Too much religion in the department stores. Hail, replica of replicas, holy smoke in a bottle for the man who has everything. Too much secrecy learned like humming in church. I'll live like a hermit among the people whose notion is Fate. Of the bill collector stumbling over the tundra, they say, "He appeared to me." They have no jokes or festivals. Their god is a fish who can hide in clear water.

Maxine Chernoff

The Unbuilding

Some say it was easy, the walls folding like tissue. But neighbors demanded, "We want more noise." The windows turned inward. Stairs tumbled like yarn. The children complained, "We want it to happen right now." Next the chimney sunk into itself like an old man singing in bed. The gutters rained nests. The fireplace sparked like news of war. "Fire is handsome," the people agreed, "unlike the unbuilding of houses."

FROM *THE TURNING* (2008)

What It Contains

Thomas contends that the novel contains scenes of violence and the detailed description of a sexual assault on a young boy.

Indeed, the novel contains one of the earliest discussions of how the conditions of slave life might be ameliorated.

In addition, the novel contains the revelations of a few hitherto well-guarded secrets.

Although the novel contains adult language and situations, it will appeal to all audiences.

The novel contains many scenes of characters being compelled to write "the truth."

The novel contains many descriptions of mouth-watering food that at the same time can be seen as homely and erotic.

In support of the pessimistic perspective, the novel contains many truly dark moments to offset the colorful ones.

As usual with Irving, the novel contains some brilliant moments of cultural observations.

But the novel contains the parallel and contrasting love of Konstantin Levin.

The novel contains a great deal of religious imagery.

The novel contains several bullfighting references, especially in the name of Tess's boat *Quernica* (the spot in the ring where the bull feels protected).

The novel contains a large amount of ethnographic material to make it seem "authentic," and there is more than a whiff of authorial exploitation here.

The novel contains a complementary story: the relationship of Glen and Miriam, who are attracted to each other but always tend to resist each other.

Those who know a bit about Church history and Scripture recognize that the novel contains much error and unsubstantiated theorizing.

An interesting feature from the linguistic perspective is that the novel contains a number of 'Newspeak' words (such as *Miniluv, doublethink, plusgood,* etc.).

The novel contains a large of minor players: neighbors, coworkers, friends, relatives and other incidental participants.

The novel contains a wealth of ideas and scientific information that could spawn research that will lead to actual inter-species communication.

The novel contains many powerful vignettes, including two memorable and controversial sex scenes—a touching one between Janet and a teenage earth female.

All copies were confiscated because the novel contains descriptions of Mao Zedong's portrait being defaced.

The novel contains many different kinds of love: intellectual, spiritual, sexual, maternal. Which moves you most and why?

As the novel contains a double focus on morality and fantasy, it is also discussed as a dystopia, which is closely related to both satire and science.

It is also true that the main thread of the novel contains the love story of Chin Pao-yu and Lin Tai-yu.

Banned in Rochester, Michigan, the novel contains and makes reference to religious matters.

The second paragraph of the novel contains the same paragraph from a first-grade primer.

The novel contains several non-beautiful, even grotesque characters such as Bessie, Whitey, the pierced waitress, Judge, and Miss Ella.

Published in 1894, the novel contains brutally realistic depictions of war.

The novel contains excellent scientific details about the Everglades and their ecological diversity.

The novel contains twenty-five episodes, many of which have ludic titles.

The novel contains many descriptions of people looking at each other with anger, supplication, pity, and understanding.

The novel contains profanity and racial slurs.

The novel contains some clichés about manhood (the "real man" and his "inner red dog," for example).

What Bakhtin's concept of dialogism suggests is that we also need a book showing that every theory of the novel contains the Quixote within it.

The novel contains the first published reference to what would become *The Dark Tower* mythos, as King's uber-villain Randall Flagg is introduced.

Scenes from Ordinary Life

(Supertitles: The Love Suicides at Sonezaki [circa 1725] describe in realistic fashion a young merchant of soy sauce who commits suicide with the prostitute he loves. Chikamatsu sought in his domestic plays to depict on the stage the tragedies which occur in ordinary life rather than the mythical struggles of the gods.)

Time: 1925

Martin Heidegger: Why is love rich beyond all possible human experiences and a sweet burden to those seized in its grasp? Because we become what we love and yet remain ourselves.

Hannah Arendt: Do not forget me, and do not forget how much and how deeply I know that our love has become the blessing of my life.

(Dejection would be more vividly suggested if each in turn stood by a drooping willow when they spoke.)

Time: 1932

Hannah : I had read the fairy tale about Dwarf Nose, whose nose gets so long nobody recognizes him anymore. My mother pretended that had happened to me. I still vividly recall the blind terror with which I kept crying: but I am your child, I am your Hannah.—
That is what it was like today.

Martin: That I supposedly don't say hello to Jews is such a malicious piece of gossip that in any case I will have to take note of it for the future.

(She had gone to the entrance of the sake shop as if to strain for a glimpse of him. She strikes an attitude of anxious reflection, one hand thrust into the bosom of her kimono.)

Time: 1950

Martin: It is beautiful to *be* an "and."
But it is the secret of the goddess.
It happens before all communication.
It rings from the deep sound of the 'ou" in you.

Elfride thanks you for your wishes and sends her best. Please give your husband our best too.

(The operator holds him almost motionless for twenty minutes.)

Time: 1960

Hannah: You will see that the book does not contain a dedication. If things had ever worked out properly between us, and I mean *between,* that is neither you nor me—I would have asked you if I might have dedicated it to you.

(She sews cloth or plays a musical instrument.)

Time: 1969–1975

Martin in tableau: Letters letters letters visits.

Hannah in tableau: Visits visits letters., etc.

(The characters must suggest the world of darkness but also the inner light that guides them.)

Time: 1975

Martin: It was a merciful death. Of course, in human terms, it came too soon.

(He plays the samisen, which Paul Claudel likened to the sound of a nerve being plucked.)

Appendix:

Poem to Martin from Hannah: We'll meet in that hour
                         White lilac in flower
                         My kisses your screen
                         All you'll need. (excerpt, 1923 or '24)

Poem to Hannah from Martin: The stranger,
                         even to yourself

she is:
mountain of joy
sea of sorrow,
desert of desire,
dawn of arrival. (excerpt 1950)

(Heard on a radio. Stage empty.)

Curtain

He Picked up His Pen in Her Defense

She was said to sweat literature.

She had done a great wrong. Over a dozen people suffered.

Marriage suited her better than nakedness.

Her fingers curled around the bone of his hip.

She stood statue-like at the foot of the scaffold.

I loved her so much that I was glad to do it all.

The girl was Miss Chadwick, and she was from the South.

I imagined her young, raging, tearing at her bodice.

An infantile form of the dramatic seemed to drive her.

She would reject Parmenides' perennial notion that "True being is timeless."

She never wanted James to grow a day older.

He had kissed her suddenly not yet unexpectedly.

"You missed me, didn't you?" she murmured.

She was an ironing board with things thrown at it.

She placed her watch on the ground so that 12:00 was parallel to the shadow.

She had on a blouse that the police matron had lent her.

She designed the square's monumental façade as key element in its grand urban plan.

She clasped her hands deeper into her crotch.

She wanted the wit of politicians to bloom transparently.

She took those pills, the blue ones.

Almost any picture could inspire her in these invisible ways.

He signed her in, "committed her," in the harsh parlance of insanity.

She was a fit culmination of his romantic history.

She had a high fever and wasn't responding to antibiotics.

She looked around her for the last time, then descended the stairs on the arm of Uncle Tadeusz.

Her Romantic revival began in France rather than England.

She ran her ugly fingers down the page.

She was shy without the presence of her talent and found it difficult to enter conversations.

She liked that joke. She thought it was terribly, terribly funny.

She thought she was Crazyhorse.

She was scampering up the trunk of the oak in the garden.

The room (she looked around it) was very shabby. There was no beauty anywhere.

She hurriedly addressed these lines to her husband, sealed them, and left them on the table.

It was becoming confused, her breasts were heaving, the shores were splitting.

Her sense of limitations was as certain as her sense of power.

"I like you very much," she said.

Little appeared to her as new in life, little came as a surprise.

She was entirely wrong on the national question.

She mistook K's reluctance to accept B's analysis for an authentic commitment to revolution.

When she went to any asylum to observe real madwomen, she found them "too theatrical" to teach her anything.

Her heroine was an oxymoron incarnate.

She showed me her own effigy painted on a cocoa box identical to the one on which she herself was painted.

Her house stood "rigid in rigid emptiness."

She flew over a Manhattan "all awash with morals."

She was on hand when Churchill came to Hyde Park.

When she came back, blood was dripping down from between her legs.

She was overall director of the World Drug Trade.

It was scarcely a few weeks before she was married.

She had forgotten public language but not our private one.

She began to water them compulsively.

"She is our heroine," said Sergey wryly.

The third daughter, she suffered for her loyalty and lack of guile.

 But she swam. She held her breath and came up swimming.

A brief cold blaze shone from her eyes that showed volumes of scorn immeasurable.

The black water was her fault, she knew.

"I can't afford to fall in love," she said.

Even before Hollywood and stardom, she was taken in by liberals—Commies too.

"Be careful she doesn't kill you."

She was an old woman and lived on a farm near the town where I lived.

With her abundant figure and masses of corn-gold hair, she symbolized all that is worth fighting and dying for.

She burned a lot of letters, you know.

She waited inside the pause. Inside her.

Morality and law were, in her mind, essentially the same.

She tugged at her hair as if in response a bell might ring in her brain.

She died five days later.

Her family was not Jewish, gypsy, communist.

Still, she was a *little* dog, and a quiet one.

She was able to pry it out: it was a frozen slug.

She was one of the few true humans in the world.

She straddled him and prepared to make the necessary port connections.

She held a big box of pastries in her hands.

"Put this on," she said.

She could casually dispose of half her family without a second thought.

Maxine Chernoff

She brought preference to history.

You were the woman and she was the man.

It seemed that she took her waif status seriously.

She meant to find a husband.

Her magnetism had several sources.

She went to prison for pacifism, maybe.

She intimated a zone of privacy for conversation and belief.

FROM *HERE* (2014)

Prose Poems

A House in Summer

Virginia Woolf wrote this paragraph.
    —Erich Auerbach

In which a woman wonders when her son will grow taller, when the weather will clear and her husband stop throwing his negative shadow on clocks and lamps and objects as they are. Will it grow lighter despite his darkness, her eyes dry, though they are mostly dry, despite the feeling of tears welling up as she wishes for the boy to have more light.

Will the room, nature's repository of conical shells and tidy driftwood and small and radiant glass beads smoothed for centuries by water's vague intentions, have something to say about the figures that come and go, the careless boy, unhappy man and woman whose demeanor makes the room glow with the distinct light of sickrooms, though no one yet is ill—but there is the care and caution one associates with grief.

When shutters break loose and the wind does its work and the people who've shined with the moment's surprises and disappointments and failures to love quite well enough have left the room, will the wind acknowledge their vivid passing on sofas and loveseats where sand is engrained in scalloped patterns of fabric woven to resemble teardrop-shaped leaves? Will photos teeter on walls in their dampened frames or simply be stacked in boxes for relatives to take to a coach house overlooking a stand of elms on a narrow hill that deflects the wind, where someday a woman opens the box in front of her grandson who asks without much concern, to pass the day, who were these people, did you know them?

And the woman, because she is sentimental but cautious with her emotions, will say without conviction, I hear they were a family who summered at the beach, who lost their mother, who thought many things and then forgot them, who loved as well as they might, as I love you, she will tell her grandson, though not it words. She will think these words as he looks at her without knowing why her answer takes so long and when it does comes seems to acknowledge some deep sorrow of inheritance neither can understand.

If this is in a book as most things turn out to be, the woman will have read it twice: once when she was young herself, a reader whose eyes grew teary for Mrs. Ramsey and all the love in the world that gathers in unmapped corners where someone comes to stand for no good reason, and then again when she is older and knows the pleasure of overhearing in her own voice things she might have said to calm herself and soothe a boy.

Daphne

So much worse for the wood that finds it is a violin.
    —Rimbaud

You try to find the easy answer to the question of the ages, the one that recedes as all steady dreams in a house of wakefulness.

You uncover a hasty truth, a candid lie, an answer like no other shaped like a boat with bat wings and certitude. This is no fable, no nursery rhyme. It is the trees' steady progress toward a cloud made of bones and abstract longing.

Nothing in its place, no place for facts rare as birth in a banyan tree during a flood—you saw the photo in the paper and imagined the woman who had climbed so heavily upward to preserve her story past harm.

Unlike Magritte's clever pipe or the oddly postured woman in the Balthus painting flung across a piano, you are serious as summer's crazy ripeness or winter's inevitability—a. weedy patch without sun near the fence ignores both seasons.

You are a realist, saint of small remarks, hero of paper white as bone. You gesture to the moon or make a leap of faith. You honor the wood of things, the breath of things, the underlining in the script that doesn't know its own destination in the pageant of forgetting.

Forgotten, you say, to any object that offers its presence. Daphne grows so slowly you can't notice—all these years it's hidden behind other greening things. Hesitating nearby, you carve a space for apparition, a space for circumspection and regret. Without them you are nothing more than windows bracing for a storm.

Construction

> *Then the air was fully of wings, the doves came down out of the sunny blue like angels in a painting.*
> —Wallace Stegner

You try to build it with scarves and wigs, the hair of women from shrines in India cut for purity and sold for profit. You cut your nails, make sure you are clean enough, you take the scrupulous bath so you are ready for the Lourdes of chemicals, alcohol, tubes. This is the oblation, the vow not to outlast but to serve, to compensate as best you can for its eventual failure.

Bargains are different—you play tricks, crossing the road coolly in front of the barreling truck—let him dare rob you with an unplanned end. Punch lines abound—how she was hit by a garbage truck, a potato truck, at the side of a friend helping her shop that day—they were sharing an eggroll.. You laugh outrageously but not with outrage when the impossibly beautiful movie does not end as it should but just accrues endings. No editor, no discipline—allegory of your life—everyone's too, this is general—so many scenes unlit, words mumbled on tape, false starts, abrupt curtailments.

You are making a collection of homely wisdom offered like cakes at the banquet. You are a snob about offerings—so much is trivial, small as an ant crawling with a large leaf bent leftward. The braveness, the unfairness, all the ways in Tibet and Peru and with eagles or crows they topple the body to provide something more substantial than your own grief for yourself, you, the best friend you've ever had, the one who knows your lies and quibbles and times you really didn't mean it, you who had even outwitted yourself. How you'd delayed because there was something more tinged with promise, more warped by danger that drew you off course. You who threw away charts and itineraries and maps. You who said no and no thank you at best.

You have no menu. You have *this* with the cube for the day, the rectangle for the week, the larger square of the month that marks a time for flags, a day for fathers, a festival in a South Asian atoll, a calendar whose photo of mountains that seem celestial are merely granite and water condensed into snow. You have minutes of still being yourself, if shadow is you, if your hand holds a lime-green glass and takes a long sip you feel deep in your throat.

It's finally not about you, but what others will say, what they whisper about the self that you weren't, all the same, really. You were quiet or self-composed, cheerful or foolishly so, alert till the end or unfeeling as ice. You are elsewhere, doubled, halved and zeroed. Maybe you can report by letter or note or an oddly voiced message that you are with yourself elsewhere or nowhere, you have what you need. Not pinned to a board in a small room without windows or sewn on a jacket, not on a booklet with dates and a line and a face with your own flaming eyes and longish chin—no harm meant in the modesty of missing, in the simply lucid sense of being here but also unseen.

COMMENTARY

U R my service dog UR white graffiti in the white bathroom of the Snow King UR a man and a woman wearing leather at a funeral for a colonel in the Russian army UR one of us UR a gun in a church UR Allen Ginsberg so lonely that you write *Howl* and *Kaddish* because you have no one to love you UR listing UR sinking UR are a fly ball hit off the bat of someone in stripes Everyone wants to sleep with you UR in the army of a neutral nation a fake army that shoots fake bullets at birch

UR my mother in a crazy dress and an empty smile and stockings with seams UR my father in a car hitting the wall of a factory at 8 a.m. on Thursday, October 17, 1974 LOL UR no one I know UR the last good wish I wished you (LOLLOLLOL) and then you were not there

UR the baby I had, three in all, the magic number that makes up the trinity of snack crackers the trinity of bones of saints the trinity of thesis synthesis trifecta I lost the race I lost the horse I watched the horse running so fast her hoof fell apart She was a great filly they said the horsemeat butcher was closed for summer Baudelaire's drainpipe was very beautiful The swan stole our baguette The park (according to the film we saw later) was full of prostitutes According to the film we saw later the initiation process must happen in Europe in World War Two and involve a slightly ugly and dim-witted boy who turns out to be funny and handsome and then dies Emily Dickinson's parking meter is set on out of time—truly, you don't believe me please do She became a heroin addict and kept a pygmy rat in her room at college She became a nurse and killed sleeping patients with morphine She became the smooth hair of a sad woman in my class who plagiarized poems and reports and thought I didn't know She became my doe-eyed student who disappeared but not in body She became my mother with her vampire lips in the photo before the war

She became a priest on holiday with dandruff and a penchant for escargots She became a Byzantine icon artist a pubic sculptor a little girl with one braid cut off by my friend in first grade She became a porn star who opened a restaurant in Northridge CA She became the only postmodern painting in Slocum Nevada She became the postscript to me she became me LOLLOLLOL

I am writing this knowing that it is first excessive and second unimportant I am writing this knowing that you may not approve of my sudden burst of prose at the end of a book of poems LOLLOLLOL which I used to think meant lots of love

Lots of love and BTW it means more, it means less, it means when you fly, I will try to join you in the vee-shaped clouds over the opera version of "Three Sisters" He says he saw a boring play with people talking I didn't understand it was "Three Sisters" who never leave and never stop talking until much later Trashy novels are the only ones that work It will not save you to write poems that save you I saw the girl to whom I once gave a B+ for not listening to me She deserved a better grade for not listening because she didn't listen so very well She was whole-hearted in her non-listening She broke the mold of non-listeners

If you were a cantaloupe, what would I be? If you were a mollusk, where would I sleep? If you were a tank, would I ride in your dark and steamy chamber?

Kings summon us and we come We are supplicants all in search of something to worship in a peculiar and profane way The Duke of Bavaria was an asshole he was worse than George Bush II maybe and maybe not LOLLOLLOL The king of Belgium thought his private factory was the Congo their trees his baubles You may lose life and limb if your mother has you in the wrong bed you may lose more if your mother has you with the wrong man we all lose everything eventually but the stories have different weight over time some are told and some are not some are redacted and blurred by water or tears or another liquid Where can I buy some fire? Where is the fire store in this mall? We do not know how to properly use things but use is of no use and value of no value My grandson eats worms and swears to their goodness It is protein I say we all need it daily My love is a white birch my love is a flower

Can you say the fucking name of the flower I ask her don't say those flowers with the white petals and the yellow center, say daisy, damn it, I tell her and she says that is elitist as is the word *imagery* Okay, let's call it vapor or if that is too abstract let's call it sidewalk Is sidewalk elitist? Is garbage elitist, or do you prefer the word *refuse,* which is easily misread Multiple readings, are they allowed here? Do I get to keep my marbles, my beautiful tiger's eye and turquoise the color of our planet? What must I surrender to get out of here? Do you need it all or just most? I will give you most without you asking I will give you all if I can LOLLOLLOL I have nothing and still have my integrity she said my justice he said my last word

It rained frogs in the movie. It rained cheddar cheese. It rained a big moon with a hole bitten through. How can you count it or sum it, the teacher once asked Say ask for a question not said Why were all teachers so sad in that building? Was it a sad building? Who drank the most, Mr. Larson or Miss Weatherbee, I swear that was her name She ran the Daniel Burnham speech contest which I lost when the bell rang and I forgot the rest of my speech like magic We were mean We were children We did not know

What is the sum of three gentlemen in a gondola? What is the sum of our natural inclinations toward deification of otherness? What is the sum of our woes? LOLLOLLOL

OFFERINGS

> *A cluster of belfries encants the human idea.*
> —Rimbaud

The heart-shaped meteorite is not message or omen, talisman or cure.

Locket of the world's intention, correlation of tangent and bone:

The church in Bruges where the blood of Christ thickened in a vial is chained to a priest.

Death on vacation, a humid Sunday when he says something trifling,

then looks at her for the final time. Who notices that a train leaves unless it is bound for grief?

The man who said he'd been blinded but now could see had kept the knowledge of failing to himself.

His blue eyes told of the miracle, which meant he would keep reading Yeats to students who Twitter and text during his lectures, who read box scores and Google their names.

Heart from the sky, blood in the vial, fragments of what's said,

left over beauty on a train to Bruges become story by connecting the dots:

Words flee, wanting a home in another context. Let's build

a reliquary where, under indigo velvet and gilded lining, they can escape prying eyes.

The Staggering Man

A staggering man is carrying a salad across the street.

This is not the first line of a word problem about velocity or distance.

I am waiting for him to cross and we have locked eyes.

He is grimacing or smiling at me. I am smiling back.

This man has a disorder that makes his case singular. It has a name and prognosis.

He is one of a galaxy of staggering men whose provocation is unclear.

I have seen them stagger in other arenas, and I have ignored their staggering in moments of disregard.

The staggering man is finally across.

My pen is out of ink, and I am writing with a crayon I found inside the seat, turquoise I would say, but Indian blue its appellation, perhaps about the ocean.

I haven't written so many poems since my twentieth year when my professor said that he

doubted a girl with my large intelligence but emotional restraint could write a single word

It sounds as if he was unkind, but his was a kindness to me, a mirror to hold up to my shadows.

The staggering man has receded.

The afternoon is brilliant with invented weather and sky-framing clouds. Several pigeons are harassing a dove, which one of my students has told me is just a smaller, dumber pigeon.

How are you today, my dear? Are you being viewed by someone who locks eyes with you and loves you? Have you read my parable and noticed its small devices?

Will you judge me with a deeper love than I could offer the staggerers and plaintiffs earlier in my years and see how I see your eyes in their reasons?

Gesture

the fabric I ate / and ate.
—Lisa Fishman

You are the one who lived beyond this and that, whose face was a recompense like a photo showing unknown people in a better time when snow covered most of the view they were trying to obscure, and smoke the rest, the beautiful variety of white smoke (maybe steam) with its waving tangents ascending to the cobalt dome of the sky.

You made televisions mad with war go blank or showed music that covered the news of more deaths here and certain lack of life there, you were with the white piano on fire and the candles blazing on the piano on fire, and on the lawn there were birds of various black hues with beaks cracking tiny yellow seeds, also there to distract you from the war.

You are the crack in the ceiling she noticed when he was not there, not in bed this night or that night, nor present in the morning. The curtains' breeze was static and the trees buzzed with peculiar light as she traced the sheets and shadows on walls and asked time to assist the process of slow forgetting which is similar to remembering but in muted, kneeling tones.

You are the record player for "my funny valentine" in this version and that version and some versions yet to be made by DJs who will break the song in half or quarters or sixteenths or forty-eighths and place parts of it elsewhere like leaves dried in books about the Moors and sing something else that reminds you of summer in Dallas or Prague or Vermont.

You are the locus of happiness locus of sorrow you are the water where dolphins nurse their young and the water that makes boats list in

Maxine Chernoff

Williams' poem "The Yachts" which is not nearly his best with its driving rhythms and forced endings and endless triumphs—he is better on small projects as you are in making happiness a temporary patch in regard for the moment and nothing to follow.

You are the formlessness of form as it breaks from its song or shape or recent invention in independence from what surrounds it, the figure that goes from one shadow to the next without disputing its small place in the painting where men come and go and sell things packed on camels in a desert that reaches beyond the castle at the end of the Silk Road and the three subsequent left turns to the ancient widow's house.

You are the eventual practice of learning to wait by a pond as light changes from morning to day to generation to others at the same pond on a Saturday late in summer when she takes his hand and he breathes in deeply and tells her to come away from here, the edges are dangerous and far too filled with memory.

You are you turning back on yourself like a dress unsewn and unraveled and no longer quite cloth—more like paper—in a narrow closet where people leave things when they move and light slants as is its tradition in rooms that get lost in a story of leaves and seasons and long endings in patience-filled sunlight.

Evidence

> *To philosophize is to learn how to die.*
> —Montaigne

Of houses, empty or noticed, to rooms whose lamps have left their light behind, ancient after time has landed in the breech of its excess, dropped there as if a package fell from the arms of a woman.

Of glasses once filled whose essence is left in a stain that looks clear in most light but carries a tinge of its erasure when she notices it late in the night after he is asleep.

Of windows, whose eyes are shut to the diversions of their intended gazers, birds passing on their sheer migrations over oceans filled with brine.

Of gardens where he sat or she sat amid the trickery of a season and its aftermath, patchy on the lawn and patchy in the sky, gray and listless for a time before respecting the progress of feeling as it overtakes the geography of plants.

Of reasons which fill a space but not adequately, which stretch like deserts between needs vocalized or calmed, written or whispered, answered or forgotten by the time an answer is prepared.

Of books filled with language that is never proper to the moment but serves as a repository of the possible though the possible is not enough, as a tent is never enough in a storm.

Of eyes that fill with knowing or restless asking or a glance that means retreat or surrender or that a village lies in waste, a life is lost, small as a child's attempt to capture a mote of dust above his bed in moonlight from a gibbous moon

Maxine Chernoff

Of melodies whose notes contain the promise of an answer, as if music is an answer or patience a virtue or love an antidote.

Anosognosia

God knows where I am.
   —Linda Bishop

Give up your princely crown: you never had it, your kingdom, your horses made of fire and tears. Give up your plans to sail the ocean in a vessel made of clouds and glue.

You are not you, not yourself, not the one whose whispers were heard by the teacher even when your lips were closed and your shiny boots on the ground. You are not the one heralded at the refuse dump by the seagulls whose cries were also the cries of a little girl dropped in a well.

You are not the handsome stranger who is awaited in the house where thirty-nine apples are rotting near the sink drain and the woman lies on the floor almost dialing a number in Connecticut of a relative whose hands were too large and too close.

Give up your jewels, the glass brooch in the shape of Siam, where you once ruled a gaggle of women who praised you in eight languages and shared your shadow with no one. Give up your heraldry and your whispered treasons by the site of the buildings that once stood as an outline even on coins.

You are not the child in the closet pretending to be the ghost of Julius Caesar. You are the lady on the bus in rags asking for pennies because she is building a ladder taller than a northern pine that will reach beyond her most feared cloudburst.

You are not the comfort of a room where she rocked and held her child before she heard it tell her that treason was in the air, that the room was filled with dirt, that a certain chief of state had it in for her unless she enunciated correctly and plainly on a certain Friday before Flag Day the names of all the ghosts and saints beginning with K.

Give up your plan to beat the dead at their game of cards, your plan to conquer Las Vegas with your lamé gown and tulle, your plan to grace the state dinner for the King of Nubia with your crown of gold thorns and thistles from your neighbor's yard.

You are not someone with a plan; you are a woman made of bone and lace, a woman made of iron and nakedness, a woman made of words and excuses for them, you are under their care, you are subject to a plan that will enable you to be among them, to gather stars if you wish but keep them secret.

Parade

The laughter of those missing/makes it clear ...
    —Bei Dao

Is it the beginning or end of the story when the road turns southward into nothing and a coyote is seen on a hillside above the tract houses and the fund-raising march approaches the house where she died last night quite late after a short illness?

She is no longer there, cushioned in moonlight, no longer a prime number, proof of her son's voice when he called for comfort the day he discovered his heart could break.

Not present for endless war and sorrow, which she will happily miss, not in the audience but in a solitary role she would mock were she asked. Who asks? Who speaks of her in the garden of the neighbor she barely knew who has become responsible for mortality as it relates to their cul-de-sac?

The neighbor's husband knows it uplifts her to care about strangers, contains her as the uncontainable leaks from the television into their ears. He remembers "The Enormous Radio," from which Cheever's protagonist hears all the tawdriness of strangers. He has learned to console her anonymous grief far better than her inventory of harms, mostly related to him.

The fund-raisers wear pink. A hideous parade outside his window. The new widower hears a megaphone tell the group of women and a few sad men that every step helps the living remember.

Her death is excluded, her death like scrimshaw, rare carving in ivory, he thinks, souvenir of vanished time that won't hold value. Is the

Maxine Chernoff

daytime moon in a phase he's never noticed, white and jagged as a paper cut?

Aversions

> *Pray Heaven that the inside of my mind may not be exposed.*
>   —Virginia Woolf

An aversion to Viennese music, the type she heard in her youth at the great amusement park by the dying green river, where all the swallows nested nearly on top of one another under a bridge and scared her with their dense blackness. Why it was the pipes of the organ that frightened her more she was unsure; perhaps the brash and hollow sound of the low notes felt oddly like wind in a desert though she had never been to a desert—or cold touching her skin at night as she changed positions in her child's narrow bed.

He was terrified of bees in any form, forms of honey, the names would throw him into a panic; clover honey, Tupelo honey, pine, whipped or combed. *Who whipped or combed it,* he wondered. And the bees' regurgitation of the nectar, the stickiness of the product, as if one could get oneself entangled finger by finger in its goldenness. As to seeing the bee itself, he would wait until dark to take walks to a bench under the elders where he'd read books on Vikings and space aliens, who had nothing to say about honey.

Her fear of cloth made it very hard for her to concentrate at the shirt factory. The bright fibers gleamed, the stripes a sin in themselves of color and pattern and roads she had forgotten to take when she'd left him. One would have brought her to a different city where she could have worked as a maid, perhaps, but then there'd be laundry and sheets; or maybe as a baker, but the flour would get sifted and poured and rolled into a perfect rectangle of significance, nearly substantial as cloth. Anything but the hum of the sewing machine on her table and the one next to hers, where the girl with the extra finger sewed even more slowly than she and whistled as he did, a melodic low tone like the kettle beginning to boil the morning she had left him for good.

His first memory of his mother's arms couldn't have been at as early an age as he imagined. Most sources say one's true memories don't exist before kindergarten. But he knew he had seen her look away when she gave him the bottle, her sunlit blue eyes blank as water. She wanted to be elsewhere, he realized, and thought for her of places that would have easily outdone the holding of this small bag of bones—what a skinny, unattractive baby, people had said, thus the supplemental bottles of a mixture of pure cream and goat's milk. He dreamed they sailed off together in a little white boat on a vast calm sheet of blue sky, he and his mother floating out of reach of the doctors and nurses and allusions of his failure to thrive that had made her so sad and unconfident.

Together they hated any type of berry. Summer was worst when the stores filled with the patriotic colors of the fruit, their reds and blues, their small variation from Sweden, the lingonberries of Ingmar Bergmann, the gooseberries of Chekhov, orbs and dents and pure circularity. Neither was allergic—they concluded that the first time they met at a picnic where they sat like sad leftovers next to a plate of creamed corn. On Thanksgiving they made the usual feast, but they were so in love they barely ate—the turkey they had roasted for so long sat on the table looking as it had been buffed to brightness. While in bed in a blissful tangle of ankles and thighs and arms, what they thought most about was their delight in having excluded cranberries from their plates. By spring it was over. The stirring they'd felt that summer in the berry aisle amid the lushness flown in from three countries on two continents was now a steely indifference, an aversion to one another, as if even a touch might elicit a cry of pain or a reverse of joy so sharp it would cut them. One night she almost ate a strawberry to declare independence from him but refrained at the last second.

Under the Music

Under the music, a baby cries in the audience. A police siren meets a thunderclap meets quantum theory.

Under the music you are falling into a sleep so calm that your face becomes architecture, your head and arms a latitude. Knees bend, and you breathe an intelligence heard in the room's soft air.

It is May here, the third month of spring. Already flowers die and new ones approach life, prodigious in their powers. Tendrils reach from under fences. Hands touch.

We build fences and sandbag rivers. We launch drones that fly crookedly toward their targets, launched by boys one might have taught beadwork at scout camp.

You stand there, lovely in your harmlessness, gazing at a neighbor's fence, where a Steller's jay rips at a tissue. New jasmine twines over older vines. Nothing can stop it, not even your concern for its reaching.

Purchase

You think it's a dream that you chop down trees in a vacant room, part of a house whose roof is treetops.

Lilies overtake the more famous flowers. Is it life when flies buzz over blurred leaves? Words prefer the color of bees.

Is it a painting when the night swirls close and you hear the beaks and tongues of birds at your neighbor's pond where an egret perches on a stone eating koi?

You are water frozen and unlabeled. What you leave of yourself gets remembered as the wobble, stare, or remnant when you turn to look and touch his skin in the blue room softened by spring.

Kindness is amplitude of attention, always the distance of reason and retort as intention dims. Vermeer's corners, famous for their absence of color, shine like a lamp in your favorite midnight room. Figure and ground seized by attention—what you want is here and here.

One practical gesture leads to another. A hand closes. An eye sees the fraying darkness and its cover of recognition.

Word

You are offered a window or widow, a Coptic stance, a bed of lightning, angels scarred by conclusions. All that escapes is matter seeking matter seeking redemption.

Under the cover of lawns in summer, angels scarred with conclusions, a hum of parasols from the pointillist past when the world was picnic and soft intention.

You are left to marshal the parade, to transcribe the waves when they encounter a body or driftwood resembling her face.

A trance envelops the flagpole, a layer of mist sinks under the headlights as they race toward a desert where a filament of reason perhaps lies under a stone.

Don't breathe a name under cover of winter stars. Don't witness the opening of grace as it descends on the two who sit calmly by the lake.

You are not yourself as a stone is itself, as a match has potential, as an idiosyncrasy contains the necessary crease in the story.

The story exists for you alone. It is not your raft or transparency, carpet or dome

In a place you once stood, water finds its level and trails off into a sentence.

Maxine Chernoff

Singular

High-mindedness is a construct of mind and its metals, its iron and zinc, its blue mercury.

It is a waste to consider how we relate to the human condition—we are the human condition in cotton and lace and charms that fit in thimbles. We are broken and fixed. We are mended and torn. We are the underlining of the soft belly of kangaroos crossed with examination books. We tell jokes that aren't funny and laugh with our eyes closed. When we open them, someone has died and another been born.

We praise Jove. We praise Allah. We praise the mark-downs at the Nordstrom Rack where a handsome young woman was weeping into her hands. We praise the immaterial essence of clouds that resemble your uncle on Wednesday. We praise the material grace of your hand on my collarbone, soft in its landing there.

We are unkind to our neighbors. We cheat on our friends. We are witnesses to the first bee in the jasmine we planted at noon. We are witnesses to the harms of a life and its slow repetitions that lead to new beauty. We travel to see peasants enact old rituals that we would find foolish in our own doorways. We are peasants as well under our skirts and children and finally fools. Who knows the height of a well-built arch or the dimensions for travel to Mars? They say if you fly there, you cannot return. There are those who will fly there. I heard them on a show discuss how they'll grieve for irises and children and the small fond expressions of those that they love.

We all leave cathedrals and ashes and bony candles burnt to their wicks. We all leave nothing we wanted and everything we did and that of an in-between state of a small conversation involving the beauty of spires.

We are not jugglers. Planes fall and leaves too and nothing that crashes or lands without sound gets repaired. Our ankles have sight of the horizon of small endings. We look forward to more as we leave more behind.

When my mother was dying, she asked, "Will I live?" I remember the silence as she turned from our silence to make herself ready, the quiet of an afternoon in a room where light and sound were present but respectful. I remember the quiet later that day as we stood alone with her. Absent at last, she withdrew with a tact saved for endings.

Please save me from all that I know must follow. Please give me a book or a song or a look that means less.

Maxine Chernoff

DRONES

> *Operators fly the planes from air-conditioned trailers thousands of miles from the war zone.*
> —*Time* magazine article

Porch lights appear—it is 1962 when the woman wearing a pink chemise retrieves the newspaper from her lawn.

We settle on news of our day, how video games have turned deadly, how children have learned the ready skills of removal.

A book's pages blow from middle to end to beginning. Nothing passes or ends. Nothing claims the text's attention. Words float upward, launched by hands.

The usual mixed with the strange is the stuff of dreams, the stuff of waking to distinctions sharp as paper, soft as candles. Far beyond shadows, a light whose origin is mystery; a new sense of the word means death, sudden as music.

Maps suggest the land has no boundaries, countries no borders. Objects of interest move on a grid: men and women, cattle, and a stray goat with stone-colored eyes.

The ache of the past connects to the present—how doorbells used to ring and strangers call. Fear was small and hovered on lips. Olives floated listlessly in drinks as people whispered local scandal in front rooms blue with information.

Surgeons of excision, men enact death's plans. Its subtlety knows no limits; out-manned and outmaneuvered, we practice remembering.

Stereopticon

From the outside, I suppose I look like an unoccupied house.
  —Wallace Stegner

No one questions the future's glass-bowl seers, the chemical air of sorrow or whorl of plastic forming the ocean of scraps. Noisy birds witness a day familiar or vague, crisp as a leaf or filled with slate-roofed clouds. Someone says *disaster.* Another cries mercy as prayers are balanced on pillows. The tragic comes to pass signaled by continual construction, by dead bees in autumn, by "answering the letter means I am lost, love," in reference to the almond trees near the gate where he stood among dappled gardens near a trellis that leaned like a private idea. Rowboats like slippers filled the harbor on a Sunday, and a small man waved from a perch on the pier, his flags and whistles tied to a board next to the sign for ultimate cures. The woman seated in the wagon felt air on her hands. A horse observed a moth pass under the arch in the square. Her small basket was dropped and fingers retrieved her beads, grace near an orchid and stone carved with numbers. He was holding a book when the ninetieth day of summer passed without remark, when the tiny globe on the three-legged stool shook, its world underwater, just as dust floated over darkly etched branches.

Stereopticon

Rowboats like slippers fill the harbor. Lights bob like lemons on water. The ninetieth day of summer passes without remark. Under the sign for ultimate cures, amber bottles with dry, suspicious corks balance on a shiny plank. Near a trellis that leans like a private idea, he pauses by the almond trees teeming with bees and finds a stick whose underside reveals decay in the greenness of August. His future holds no promise. He lays down his book of curious beasts. He likes the snake-headed woman whose shoulders are bare, except for a shawl, having found such wonders in a market thick with sugar and scarves, honey and dates, hills of coins and blue glass charms near a stone wall made in a war. He prefers evening in its hopeful shadows when old men get lost in thought. On such a night, he had first seen her in a wagon near a hexagonal marker. It seemed her arms were filled with air.

STEREOPTICON

She examines the tiny globe, world underwater, and writes slowly, "Answering this letter means I am lost, love." Dark boughs of a tree hit the side window. She imagines a rustling in all of nature, wind swarming the trellised gate where he stood among the almonds trees blossoming. He had shown her the picture of the snake-headed woman with delicate, smooth arms. He collected amber bottles from the market that summer; poison vials, he called them. He had never hoped. If bees sent him solace, if love were a cure. She found comfort in a blue door frame surrounded by the dark, ancient ivy of novels. Soon it would be winter, the harbor frozen, fish like embers under ice. *Ultimate cures,* a slogan on the pier, a trick of summer when amber shone in a window to decorate an hour.

Maxine Chernoff

Beheld

> *... gives to airy nothing / A local habitation and a name.*
> —Theseus, *A Midsummer Night's Dream*

Let us be imagined by the sympathetic eye, borders realigning, singularity lost as bees in cumulus clouds over a locus of belief. To stare at the world, thinking it fragile despite root systems deep and undismissable. To be dust under a stairwell or a book left open as one sleeps. To comfort the view and conjure grace, blessing a glass of water or a hand that finds a small, sheer ledge that yields to remembering.

Window

The actual knocks on any closed door, beggar's robe tattered, features obscured in the dark. Light clarifies an edge of knowing, secret theme left as a match near a candle. Nothing that touches another close object can keep itself whole—dust meets shadow, inscribing an arc. Dominions are small, crevice or crease in a story, parenthesis of an hour. The amaryllis grows in a day, its solstice private and ancient, flowering into the told.

Maxine Chernoff

Momentum

> *Anyone accumulates a downfall.*
> —Stacy Doris

No stranger to call or response, you wander in velocity's style through syllables of grace.

You are accustomed to fact as lie, lie as truth, encumbered beyond a sight of landing.

Under your costume you are a woman whose hair was cut short last year and remained that way.

You are her voice under her own, her taste of certain minerals harsh to the ear of promise.

Promise to waste warmth on geography, volatile intention to burn the woods, its features and maps.

Mistake's knowing face set boundaries for your own—you come in love, leave in resemblance.

AGAIN

You ride upon trestles to dream's remembered peak, where you exchange words for sentence, meaning's unholy cargo of wished endings and lofty songs. Toward the known birds of late afternoon, toward the uncertain plane of reason beyond the turn in your thoughts of brokenness or hope, there you are with your silence and breath. In a room in the house of language, you drop intention's offered theory and claim a minute's circumstance, alone at the table where apple is round and pear fulfillment.

For every appetite there is a world.
  —Bachelard

You starred in the movie with Maud Gonne and Socrates and Juliet and a flock of sparrows that were a fixed point like the spire of a cathedral but made of feathers. You were naked and clothed and wearing nothing visible except when you sat or stood or began to speak, and then the words were made of black yarn, and your fingers held them as in an outline of reverie. You were there and not there and when I partially held you, the idea of you faded into a hint of light tinged by a window in the westernmost sky. And under the window, your face was vaguer and therefore more intimate in its shadowed complexity. If water is proof of thirst and knowledge a satisfied hour with a book, then stories end as they begin at the height of invention without a suffix of time and its pressures. You starred in the movie, and certain necessities fled like figures animated by their own recognition.

Knowing

> *A secret dream of emulating the cartographer or the diamond cutter animates the historical enterprise.*
> —Paul Ricoeur

You're here on a couch, pillows fluffed, dreaming in Latin. You're in a tablet carved on a mountain and given to men whose ears filled with ontology. You're near a stream whose source is the next cogency for a traveler stunned as Hölderlin trying to remember his name. You're in the dream in which his hands are yours and conclusions marked by sighs and breathing. You are nowhere, a signal or code meant to sweep you under a wave or a cloud or a whispered veil of induction. The French Revolution began without you and ended the same. You are not needed in this chapter in which the king's clothes are described as raiment or ermine cloak. If you are required by time and its minions, you will receive notice, as spiders when the dew shakes a web and the world blinks to attention.

Maxine Chernoff

PHILOSOPHER

Followed and noticed, referenced and catalogued, perfection's garden posits its signs, in service to its acacia, loam, and dark earth beneath the milked aspens. Reentering is justice, recompense, travelers asleep with their conclusions. Aesthetics of want and labor, error and hope, wish and indifference face a more distant north. You bear translations of snow, recite prophecies of smoke, exhale all visible means of navigation beneath bright gestures. Where is your sign and your treason, your cape and your betrayal, your measure, ancient and smoother than truth? Day-blind, sleep-neared, tucked in fog, you recede as myth of birds' tender migration.

Nocturnal

> *Time and its 'It was.'*
> —Heidegger

You are not alone in the catalogue, you with your hourglass and omens, your presumptions and solos. You are a catacomb, black letters on dark stone, a series of hereafters punctuated by night's late pillow.

Another you waits like a pair of shoes on a staircase. Nothing wears its history darker than a purse of midnight, winter's hedge, astronomy's fictions. Orbit unknown, principles tossed by gravity, you are your own island, your own Egypt, speckled egg in a nest of gray feathers. Eyes attuned to life's curses and wax, its devotions and triptychs of blame. Glass stained and ripened by moonlight inscribed thus: *a pearly veil welcomes you, traveler.*

Road

The muse of forgetfulness meets the muse of forgetting on an afternoon road. They wander together until a lamp intervenes and the scene is erased.

Late December's dimness lifts the green toward sky's smooth paper. The world is a camera. Words tie you to sparrows fence-colored in gardens of nothing past its season. Evening is a charm, its gold-threaded ending lost in the story.

Edge

Under the same photo of tree with its owl, dew with its feathers, light with its obstruction of motives, you name the moment by tying it to a stone, which itself has a history before yours and future without you. Earthly life made of dirt and ashes, bones, and a cloistered devotion. Eyes blink until sleep's window parts shores. You bear witness to a dance that welcomes disclosure, as notes touch each other's edges. Subplot or subject, the story of an hour, ripeness seeks a lens to frame its arrival.

Maxine Chernoff

Here

There is a world in which the old tumult breathes its conclusions. Inside, we are purple notes and wings of doves, visibility nothing can equal, which holds us, hesitating, as if movement might break the tender chord we strike as antidote to time. Unmask me, double me, make me a tangent in your circle of radiant breath— here with you, where the said is an offering. We are reworked, the moment a measuring device and a grace note, sorrow's window closed to the view.

Nature

Redrawn with new eyes, longing erased by flower's machinery.

Nature's exit is time altered by intention, atmosphere absolute as a love letter.

Beyond the voice of language, nameless events tarnish their speaker,

depth a trick of eyes challeging mortal experience.

Too much to separate Into the marvelous and its contrivances,

knowing how it feels to own grace, then lose its location.

FROM *CAMERA* (2017)

(2:45 pm. 20 January 2014)

Preface

> *Lord, increase my bewilderment.*
> —Fanny Howe

The work of this moment: a life is celebrated and others are born and die as I write this sentence. There is the small hum of a machine that runs on the melted bones of dinosaurs and the smell of cut vegetation. There is the taste of salt on my knuckle and glaciers melting and fires in the south of my state. There are circumstances. There are feelings. There are connections to be made or not about memes and twerks and a YouTube version of Johnny Cash at San Quentin when all the prisoners were white. The work lives now and in retrospect. The work lives in an empire of great cruelty and wealth, where the average citizen is punished daily and not given what she needs (give us this day our gluten-free bread). Drones hit targets as we speak. The last bee in the garden has its singular existence as it approaches the lily and is part of a community whose existence is threatened by a plague and pesticides, and yet it cannot present its own case to the world: hence, Emily Dickinson. That is the work, giving voice to itself, holding within itself the deep notions of the moment. The work's attention is also its ignorance. The work is beyond unkind to everything it omits. The work cannot fulfill its duties of repairing the broken world all around it. The work struggles to contain itself. It does not bleed to death or get crushed by an army. The poem sucks the nectar and returns to its hive.

Maxine Chernoff

As If

if loved—could change the weather, could send aspen through rooftops and make rain, make shiny petals spin, change matter to attention. Plants blink and stars send energy toward the lonely billions, who, if loved, love as no others, love as themselves in patterns of tongue and lips, if loved send roots, send arms, send the tumbling grace of notes, if loved send grasses from brackish water toward salty air, send, if loved, attention, send, the brassy strings of noble firs and the harmonies of roots maintaining ground: all possible gatherings spring from the eye, the hand, the blessed words of vapor and truth. The hummingbird asks the flower the hour of closing, not a grief but if loved a testing.

Did I Tell You?

The Kansas City Stomp was not written in Kansas City.
　—Jelly Roll Morton

How you were made of words on a lazy Sunday when letters hovered, birds against winter's white. On the borders of a page the indifferent field was absent of decorative stone, how you were an expenditure of voice and stranger still, said nothing. Born of time and its corrections, memory's trapdoor, the song is a limit, the smallest bridge to the next hesitation.

Ballad

> *An ethereal wind chorus opens the second scene.*
> —Stanley Sadie

Recumbent this October without fog, without robes of silk tied across the sky, the white of a wing is strange in this air. The sanctity of an hour is crystalline response, as we place our kindest selves in the world, which wears our sorrow as a lover the scent of her beloved. How we wrest distance from its map to reach the radiance of late flowers, funereal in color, ordinary as containment. Place me in the earth, and I will breathe for days. Lock the doors to the actual and the world will mime its calm retreat into dusky grapes and glistening bell.

Artifact

First the weighing then the grace then the reaching toward design. A future artifact knows you well, redacted zones of intimacy and ardor left for colder climes, the green notion of branches rocked by wind and growth stays whole by error, held in abeyance, reified or deified, numbered. The story travels in the longitude of seldom seen adumbrations, decoder rings, tea and letters from observers of your absence. Whole or retracted, the night gloved our hands. What did we feel holding the world wrapped in velvet?

CUCHULAIN

You wind up in limbo with liars and thieves who fear you, then sew your own shroud. The exit a portal: you must grow wings. And like crickets in season and crows at dawn, or the moss at your feet feeding the stream, you are small and of things, as if heaven or whatnot were the simple yard of a house in spring. Must you believe? In sewing, in patience, as vines cover the windows and you let them. Come in, you say, to the wind at the gate. You scatter your weakness, splayed on white sheets, no homecomings, hearth, or register. You mend what needs fixing, taking your cue from autumn's trick of divesting, here and not here at once

Acknowledgments

Gratitude to the editors of the following books:

The Last Aurochs (Now! Press: Iowa City, 1976).

A Vegetable Emergency (Beyond Baroque Foundation: Venice, CA 1977).

Utopia TV Store (The Yellow Press: Chicago, 1979).

New Faces of 1952 (Ithaca House: Ithaca, 1985).

Leap Year Day (Another Chicago Press: Chicago, 1991).

World: Poems 1991–2001 (Salt Editions: Cambridge, England, 2001).

Evolution of the Bridge: Selected Prose Poems (Salt Editions: Cambridge, England, 2003).

The Turning (Apogee Press, Berkeley, 2007).

Here (Counterpath Press: Denver, 2014).

Camera (Subito Press: Boulder, 2016).

About the Author

MAXINE CHERNOFF is a professor and former Chair of the Creative Writing program at San Francisco State University. She has edited the long-running literary journal *New American Writing* and is the author of six books of fiction and fifteen books of poetry, most recently *Camera* (Subito, 2016). In 2013 she won an NEA Fellowship in Poetry and in 2009 the PEN USA Translation Award for her co-translated *Selected Poems of Friedich Hölderlin*. Her collection of stories, *Signs of Devotion*, was a *New York Times* Notable Book of 1993. Both her novel *American Heaven* and her book of short stories, *Some of Her Friends That Year*, were finalists for the Bay Area Book Reviewers Award. Her collection of poetry *New Faces of 1952* (Ithaca House), won the 1985 Carl Sandburg Award for Poetry. She has read her poetry in Belgium, England, Australia, Germany, Brazil, Scotland, China, The Czech Republic, and Russia.

www.ingramcontent.com/pod-product-compliance
Lightning Source LLC
Chambersburg PA
CBHW020330170426
43200CB00006B/331